WHEN
Death
TOUCHES YOUR LIFE

What You Need to Know

WHEN

Death

TOUCHES YOUR LIFE

PRACTICAL HELP IN PREPARING FOR DEATH

By Mervin E. Thompson

PRINCE OF PEACE PUBLISHING
Burnsville, Minnesota 55337

Revised Edition
3rd Printing - January, 1987

Unless otherwise indicated, Scripture quotations are from the Revised Standard Version of the Bible (RSV), copyrighted 1946, 1952, © 1971, 1973 by the Division of Christian Education of the National Council of Churches of Christ in the U.S.A., and are used by permission.

Library of Congress Catalog Card Number

Thompson, Mervin E., 1941-
  When death touches your life.

  Bibliography: p.
    1. Death—Religious aspects—Christianity.
2. Funeral rites and ceremonies—United States.
I. Title.
BT825.T48   1986   248.8'6   86-544
ISBN 0-933173-02-4

Printed in the United States of America

In Gratitude
to my wife Jackie
and children Deanna & Noel
for all of their wonderful
love & support

By the Same Author
Living Stones
Starting Over Single

Table of Contents

I am especially grateful to the many people at Prince of Peace Lutheran Church who have inspired, encouraged, and supported the creation and writing of this book. Almost all of what I have learned about dying and death has come by entering into the life and experiences of the people in this community of faith. We have gone through the Valley of the Shadow on numerous occasions, wondering how we could bear the pain that was present. But we have also discovered the hope we have in Jesus Christ, the comfort and strength and power which is ours in the fellowship of believers. We are still learners, always on the way, never arriving at the point or place we hope to be. This book serves as a roadmap showing where we have been, where we are today, and where we hope to be in the future.

I was called to be the pastor of Prince of Peace Lutheran Church in Burnsville, Minnesota, in 1970. Located just 16 miles south of downtown Minneapolis, it was a congregation which was just entering a period of explosive growth. And grow we have, from around 1,000 baptized members in 1970 to over 5,000 members in 1985. Such growth has created many possibilities, and not a few problems. But it has been a very exciting place in which to live and be involved in ministry.

Prince of Peace congregation decided to relocate in the mid-70s to a place called the Ridges. The Ridges is a 120-acre site which is owned by the Fairview Community Hospital System and has been designed to be a socio-medical campus. In 1985 the complex includes a full service hospital, a nursing home, and three medical office buildings. Our church is located right in the midst of this campus, serving as the spiritual center. Within the next five years there will be high rise housing for the elderly, some residential housing, an extensive YMCA facility, and more medical office space. We find this a most exciting place.

I have always enjoyed writing and have written some articles for various periodicals, as well as numerous pieces for the church. But a turning point came for me in 1984 when a generous gift helped create the Prince of Peace Publishing Company. One of the purposes behind such an endeavor was to encourage various staff members of our congregation to do some creative writing. I was happy to respond to such an opportunity. The first book that I wrote for this publishing company was entitled *Starting Over Single*, completed in the spring of 1985. This present book will be the second.

I would especially like to thank Wayne Skaff, our business administrator, who has been the driving force behind the publishing company. Wayne previously worked in the book ministry of the Billy Graham Association, so he has an extensive background in publishing and marketing. I also am very grateful for the members of the publishing board: Jack Fenton, Gail Steel, Jim Dock, Sharon Johnston, Joel Suzuki, Howard Knutson and Dave Brandell, who have given outstanding leadership to this endeavor. A final tribute must go to Mary Jeanne Benson and Sue Swanson, who have served as proofreaders for this manuscript, and to editors Jackie Thompson and Ann Duin.

The basic substance of this book emerged from the work of a task force that was formed in the spring of 1984 at Prince of Peace. It was abundantly clear that many of the people in our community had not done much preparation for the reality of death. When such an event took place, it was devastating for all concerned. Many of us were convinced that if people had an opportunity to do some talking about death and to do some wise and thoughtful planning, then, even though death is a very painful experience, some of the trauma and heartache could be lessened. We certainly had all seen situations in which families who had experienced a death had never even talked about this possibility and had no idea what to do or where to turn.

Thus, I would like to express my admiration and thankfulness to those persons who served on this task force and gave much insight and inspiration. They include Leone Beneke, Beth Bouman, Dave Brandell, Gloria and Wayne Husby, Carolyn Johnson, Paul Ledin, Bob Mitchell, Jan O'Brien, Julie and Scott Peterson, Rick Ruckdashel, Sharon Schwenderman, and Bill and Sigrid Stone. A special word of appreciation is also in order to the director of the Burnsville Funeral Home, Greg Anderson, who was so gracious in providing necessary information and input.

When we came to Burnsville some 15 years ago, we discovered that it was very different from the established neighborhood where we had been living in Minneapolis. One of the major differences was due to the age of the residents; in Minneapolis we had been surrounded by elderly persons, but in Burnsville almost everyone was very young. We had hundreds of children, but almost no people over the age of 50.

Because of these demographics, it was not too surprising to learn that death was just not supposed to happen in our city. The majority of our confirmation students had not even been to a funeral, many did not know anyone who had died. At the same time our city did not have a hospital, a nursing home or even a funeral home. If a person became ill, or if a person died, that happened somewhere else. We were into living. Our church centered its ministry on families, baptisms, youth groups, and preschoolers. We never worried very much about the end of life. That was several decades away for most of us.

In fact, in one four-year period we did not have one funeral for a member of the congregation. Given the fact that we had more than 2,000 members at the time, it is not hard to see we were living in a fantasy world. But then all of a sudden we had four deaths in a relatively short period. People actually did die while we were in the midst of a time of denial and illusion, thinking that this could never happen. It is amazing sometimes how we are brought back to reality in a most graphic and dramatic way.

We were almost overwhelmed by the grief and sorrow and shock of these deaths among us. Not having been at all prepared for this possibility, we were totally devastated. We discovered in a painful way that our perfect little suburban community where everyone lived life to the fullest was subject to tragedy and heartache, just like everyone else. Intellectually we had known all of this, of course, but now it became a part of our very being. We had tasted the reality of death and found it to be very bitter. However, we had also discovered that God's comfort, hope, and assurance were also present. There was a tremendous outpouring of love and support at the time of death. We had far more resources than we knew, and the church was able to become a caring community. It almost took death to make us truly human.

We talked for some years about preparing a brochure to help people do adequate planning for their eventual death. Because of the age of the congregation, we had never been motivated to move on this as fast as we should have. But finally in 1984, after some sudden and unexpected deaths, we decided that the time had come to do something. Thus, we formed the task force on *Preparation for Death* and set out to provide some help for our members. It was a time of tremendous growth in awareness and sensitivity for all of us on the task force, and we were very pleased with the final product. The resulting brochure then became the foundation for the creation of this book. Copies of the brochure are available through the Prince of Peace Publishing Company, 13801 Fairview Drive, Burnsville, Minnesota 55337.

Just a final word of tribute. One of the members of the task force, Paul Ledin, discovered shortly after our work was completed that he had a brain tumor. This was a shock to all of us who had spent these many weeks talking about being ready for death. Now Paul was to face this possibility in his own life. At the same time that we were saddened by this development, we also knew from our many discussions that Paul was indeed ready. We were not ready to let him go, but he was ready, prepared to enter a new part of God's kingdom. Paul died in December, and our whole task force joined with the congregation to give thanks for his witness and wisdom among us. It is always good for each of us to be prepared.

WHEN *Death* TOUCHES YOUR LIFE

LIFE TO
THE FULLEST

*I*t may seem strange to begin a book about preparing for death with some words about life. The temptation in such a book would be for us to rush headlong into an intense and exhaustive discussion of funerals, caskets and cemeteries. We so often are convinced that we have discovered all we need to know about life; we know the secrets to abundant and fruitful living. But it is precisely as we come face to face with the reality of death that we are challenged to take a hard look at the meaning of life. To say this another way, the most productive action to take in preparing for death is to truly live life the way God intended us to live. To be prepared for the future means to truly live in the present.

Jesus provided a marvelous and unique way of responding to the major issues and questions of life. When someone pushed him for an answer, when someone pressed him for a profound or deep analysis of an issue or situation, Jesus responded most of the time with a parable. Instead of setting forth definitions or for- mulating some elaborate and complicated theological premises, Jesus told stories. He told one brilliant and moving story after another, timeless parables which speak directly to each of us even in this technological age.

It is regrettable that many sermons today do not adequately use this marvelous approach, the use of a story, to explain truth, ethics and meaning. Often we easily fall into the trap of trying to spend our time in definition and analysis, sometimes called the "paralysis of analysis". But as Jesus knew instinctively, people do not usually respond to abstract principles; they will not commit their lives to some kind of general ideal. Rather, if one or more of the stories that Jesus told can become our story, this can move and shape us in many profound and specific ways.

One of the questions that came often to Jesus had to do with the end of life. People have always struggled with the finality of death. Jesus was asked, "What is the meaning of death? What is on the other side? How can we be a part of the kingdom of God?" And Jesus responded to these questions with stories. One of the most familiar stories about the meaning of life and death is found in the parable of the rich fool, Luke 12:16-21.

"The land of a rich man brought forth plentifully; and he thought to himself, 'What shall I do, for I have nowhere to store my crops?' And he said, 'I will do this: I will pull down my barns, and build larger ones; and there I will store all my grain and my goods. And I will say to my soul, Soul, you have ample goods laid up for many years; take your ease, eat, drink, be merry.' But God said to him, 'Fool! This night your soul is required of you; and the things you have prepared, whose will they be?' So is he who lays up treasure for himself, and is not rich toward God."

This is a story about preparing for death. It is also a story of living, about life. We are so often tempted to prepare for death by accumulating things, by finding security in the sum of our possessions. But Jesus declared very clearly that security is not found in what we have, only in what God can give. *"Do not lay up for yourselves treasures on earth, where moth and rust consume and where thieves do not break in and steal. For where your treasure is, there will your heart be also"* (Matthew 6:19-21).

We best prepare for death by incorporating the priorities and and mission of Jesus into our lives. We are most ready to die when we are most involved in living for others. Thus, this chapter will be an attempt to focus on some priorities for Christian living: on balance, wholeness and integrity in living. In a sense, the kind of wholeness, the completeness we shall discuss, is beyond us; it will be present only in the kingdom of God. On the other hand, it is a goal and ideal for life and should be that for which we strive. I would challenge each of us to find the kind of life which is not only a preparation for death, but also a foretaste of the resurrected life for which we hope.

Often in the past we in the Christian community have tended to concentrate on using the word "holiness" to describe the central goal in our lives. People have been admonished by pastors time and again to live "holy" lives. There is nothing wrong with this, but in recent years there has been an increasing amount of emphasis on the word "wholeness". In essence, these two words are not all that different. They come from the same root. The problem has been that "holiness" has so often been seen as only a spiritual word or concept; to be holy has meant to live the kind of life that is almost other-worldly, separate from the world. But "wholeness" suggests that all of life is touched by the Gospel, there is nothing in our existence which is not called and changed and shaped by the person and work of Jesus Christ. Therefore, to live a life of wholeness is a radical call with powerful implications.

Wholeness

The first chapters of Genesis paint a picture of wholeness. The *Bethel Bible Series* by Rev. Harley Swiggum suggests there are four kinds of harmony present in chapters one and two of Genesis, all of which contribute to this wholness. There is harmony with God, harmony with others, harmony with ourselves, and harmony with the world in which we live. This was God's intention for each of us from the very beginning of the world—that we should live in harmony, that we should be whole, complete.

However, as evidenced by the third chapter of Genesis, this intention was dashed in the midst of humankind's quest to be like

God. Harmony became disharmony. Yet, even though we have all sinned and fallen short of the glory of God, the wholeness that was envisioned in the first chapters of Genesis is still the ideal, it is still the vision which calls and moves our lives. Harmony and wholeness are still the hope and the picture of what life is supposed to be.

Sometimes life is like walking a tightrope. Keeping our balance often becomes a full-time endeavor. There are so many forces which are seeking to break our stride, to cause us to lose our step for a moment, to push us over the side. The winds of change, temptation, and crisis often become strong indeed, pushing us one way or another. The tightrope begins to sway and tremble. We often want to reach out and grab onto some support, but sometimes that support is hard to grasp. Maintaining our balance is not an easy task.

This struggle for equilibrium and balance seems to be especially true as we seek to be faithful in our Christian journey. We almost seem to be on a balance beam, with many forces pushing and shoving us one way or the other, pushing us very close to the edge. We identify with the Apostle Paul when he wrote, *"For I do not do the good I want, but the evil I do not want is what I do"* *(Romans 7:19)*. Sometimes we know how to keep our balance, we know where to turn for support, but we simply do not want to take the necessary effort to do so. Thus we find ourselves falling.

I truly believe that most of us would love to find some kind of balance in our lives, some wholeness, a kind of beautiful harmony and peace, with everything kept in healthy perspective. That would certainly be our dream, our vision, our hope. It is frustrating and painful to consistently be out of balance, out of control. After vacationing one summer in Colorado and spending a few days living at an altitude of over 9,000 feet above sea level, I suffered some disturbing side effects after returning home. It seemed as if the world was often spinning, as if everything was out of balance. I could not focus on the needs and tasks of the moment. I can attest to the fact that it is extremely frustrating to be out of balance.

Lives which are balanced and harmonious are most often far more productive than those which are out of focus. This is what the Holy Spirit is about in our lives, calling us to a life of harmony and wholeness. In this chapter I would like to concentrate on four areas of life where wholeness is so important and to give some suggestions on how to keep these in balance. We always remember that we cannot do this balanced life alone, but only by the power of the Holy Spirit, and the love, concern and encouragement of our Christian brothers and sisters. To find wholeness is to become more of what God has intended us to be.

1. Wholeness of the Body

Paul writes these words of challenge to each of us: *"I appeal to you therefore, brothers [and sisters] by the mercies of God, to present your bodies as a living sacrifice, holy and acceptable to God, which is your spiritual worship" (Romans 12:1).* Present your bodies as a living sacrifice.

That Paul would place such a high priority on taking care of the body may surprise us. In his time, long before jogging, health clubs, and diet centers became popular, you would expect him to be more concerned about the inner life of the spirit than the care of the body. But Paul talks about the worth, the value and the care of the body on more than one occasion, even describing the Christian journey as being like a race, where we discipline, train and develop the body to its limits.

Renewal and wholeness have a great deal to do with the body, as well as with the rest of our personhood. I remember some years ago attending a weekend retreat which was designed to be a time of renewal and refreshment. But it turned out that most of the two days were spent in meetings, sitting for hour after hour in sharing times. In addition to this, we were given three very rich and filling meals, with dessert. What I discovered was that the overall experience unbalanced us, for we had devoted virtually no time to taking care of the body, to exercise. I have become a firm believer that any retreat or renewal experience needs to have some kind of strenuous physical activity as well as times for the mind or the spirit.

A confirmation of this truth for me came when my wife Jackie and I spent a few days at a resort in beautiful northern Minnesota. It was a lovely spot, with rooms and dining room overlooking a breathtaking lake. But we discovered that the only place for exercise was to walk on a heavily traveled road. It was nice for a few days to just sit and unwind, but we soon discovered that true renewal takes place not only in relaxation and contemplation, but also in exercise.

We made a commitment that in the future we would vacation in a place having ample opportunity for physical exercise. Most of our favorite vacations have offered hiking in the mountains. To find wholelistic renewal for us involves more than just lying on the beach or sitting in the dining room.

Part of our problem in the Christian Church is that we have often given mixed signals concerning the body. Some of the confusion has come from a misinterpretation of the person and humanity of Jesus Christ. Martin Luther in his *Small Catechism* writes, "I believe that Jesus Christ, true God, son of the Father from eternity, and also true man, born of the Virgin Mary, is my Lord." Jesus is true God and true man.

What has happened is that many people down through the years, especially theologians influenced by Greek thought, believed that Jesus could not have been truly human. He did not have a physical body because the body was supposed to be evil, worth little or nothing. Who cares about the body? Only the mind, the soul and the spirit were important. Life here on earth was just a time that would pass quickly. He would soon ascend to that wonderful place where the spirit would be separated from the rather disgusting body.

Thus, for all those who were influenced by this line of thinking, Jesus could only have been true God. He would never have even considered becoming a human being, being one of us. This is exactly the issue John is addressing when he begins his Gospel with the words, *"In the beginning was the Word, and the Word was with God and the Word was God" (John 1:1).* The Greeks could accept these words of John—the Word, which is the Logos, was in the beginning with God. "Amen," said the Greeks.

But then, in John 1:14, John writes the revolutionary words, *"And the Word [the Logos] became a human being and dwelt among us, full of grace and truth, and we beheld his glory, the glory of the Father."* Amazing. Unbelievable. The Word of God became a human being, a body. Jesus was true God and true man.

We are not, therefore, just disembodied spirits, but our bodies were created in the image of God, and have infinite value, dignity and worth. God created human beings, he created bodies, and saw that his creation was very good. We are not only body, we are indeed very human.

In addition, we seem to be rediscovering the meaning of Baptism in this period of our history. Whenever we talk about this Sacrament we must remember that it takes very seriously the value of the body. You don't usually pour water on a spirit; rather you sprinkle or immerse a body, in our tradition usually a precious, squirming, beautiful little baby.

A Roman Catholic parish in our area is now beginning to experiment with immersion in the Sacrament of Baptism, after not practicing this for many centuries. The priest takes the baby and dips the child into a little tank that has been constructed for this purpose. The whole body is immersed, and in a sense they are trying to affirm the words of Paul, *"Present your whole body as a living sacrifice, holy [wholly] acceptable to God" (Romans 12:1).*

I must admit that I am probably not the right person to talk about wholeness in terms of the body. I simply do not take care of my own body as I should. I must confess that I am a compulsive eater, I do everything wrong when it comes to the ingestion of food. I eat too fast, I eat for the wrong reasons: nervousness, stress, excitement, and habit. I have a weakness for Big Macs, Dairy Queens, cashews and pizza. There are times when I eat more junk food in a day than I should eat in a month.

I am not happy with myself when I do this, when I "pig out", and I have this continuing conversation with myself: "Merv, you are a reasonably intelligent human being, you have demonstrated some willpower in certain areas of your life. Why don't you eat properly and exercise regularly? You are so often out of control." I know something of what an alcoholic goes through and often think of the words I read some years ago by Paul Tournier, "Most people do not die, they kill themselves." Stress, lack of exercise, diet, alcohol, smoking, and other factors do play a major part in harming the body.

It is one thing to know all this, however, and another thing to do it. I have a difficult time staying on the balance beam. Thus, Paul's words have important relevance, *"Present your body as a living sacrifice, holy and acceptable to God."* When our body is out of control in any way, it is very difficult for the rest of us to be in focus, in harmony, in balance, to be whole.

One other word should be noted about the body, this coming from a completely different context. The movie industry and television have really done a number on us. Day in and day out we see the abuse of the body going on right in front of us. It is the new morality, or perhaps the old where the body is out of control. "Liz is to marry Number Eight" screams the headline, someone else marries Number Four, and most don't bother to get married at all. The media seem to present one serial marriage after another, as people move from one partner to another as soon as the honeymoon is over.

It all looks so glamorous, so chic—turn in the old model for a new one. I have a poster containing a picture of four healthy-looking cows, all of them standing in fields of lush grass. Separating each of the cows from the others is a barbed wire fence. But each of the cows has its head in the next pasture, trying to graze where it is not supposed to be. This illustrates that the grass always seems greener somewhere else. We believe there is something profound and exciting that we are missing, some ecstatic sexual experience to be found just over the next fence.

However, I would like to take anyone who is tempted by this illusion on a journey around our community, or any other locale, and invite them to listen to the stories of so many who believed this new morality would be the gateway to happiness. I would like to introduce each of us to the people who have swallowed the line of the television preacher who promises, "You can have what you want, when you want it, all the time." The heartache and pain in the lives of those who have chased this rainbow is beyond measure.

If we wonder sometimes whether there is a hell, just listen to a person who chose to have an affair, who has decided that the commandments are just not applicable anymore in this sophisticated age, who has spent his or her own version of the mid-life crisis chasing after some forbidden fruit. Then, after you have listened to all of the tears and pain, the remorse and guilt that comes pouring out, you will know again that the Bible has not been whistling in the dark. *"Present your bodies as a living sacrifice, holy and acceptable to God" (Romans 12:1).* The first part of wholeness has to do with the body.

2. Wholeness of the Mind

Paul goes on to say in Romans 12:2, *"Do not be conformed to this world, but be transformed by the renewal of your mind, that you may prove what is the will of God, what is good and acceptable and perfect."* Remember the mind to keep it holy, or whole. I wonder sometimes if this area of ourselves has not been neglected even more than the body.

In modern day America we have all sorts of opportunities for the care of the body — health clubs, Weight Watchers and jogging paths. But there is very little around to help shape up the mind. So often the temptation is to just sit in front of the tube and let the mind dangle. I have this sinking sensation that most people do not read anymore, except to inhale material which is a cross between romance paperbacks and *People* Magazine.

I am particularly concerned about children, especially with small boys, although with equality being a current theme, we are rapidly bringing little girls on board as well. In many communities today we have brainwashed so many of our children to believe that meaning and fulfillment in life come through constant participation and excellence in athletics. From the time many of them are out of diapers, they are chauffeured, controlled, challenged and pressured into becoming athletic phenomenons.

As a result, many of our young people can run faster, hit a ball farther, throw better and skate more proficiently than any generation in history. Yet many of these young people can hardly read and have spent virtually no time in the renewal of their minds. They can bring great joy to athletic coaches and some ardent parents, but their English teachers are appalled, and they are unbelievably ill-prepared for life after high school.

To capture the sense of a wholelistic lifestyle means to take the development of the mind seriously. This is what led Paul to write, *"Be transformed by the renewal of your mind"* (Romans 12:2). It is in the mind that the life-changing decisions are made. It is the mind that brings reason and rationality to bear in such a multitude of situations. It is the mind which needs to be challenged by the intellectual demands of the Gospel of Jesus Christ. When our minds are completely dominated by such things as tax shelters, athletics and color of the new wallpaper, then we are out of touch with those things which are eternal.

I talked with a college student recently who is reading books by great authors, such as *Crime and Punishment* by Feodor Dostoevski, *Death of a Salesman* by Arthur Miller, *No Exit* by Jean Paul Sartre, *Denial of Death* by Earnst Becker. This simply brought home to me how shallow my own reading often becomes, how easy it is to let the mind go to seed. I am almost embarrassed to admit that the last two books I have read were written by Andy Rooney and Erma Bombeck.

The Christian faith is meant to challenge our minds. It is meant to change the whole person by the changing of our minds. If it is "garbage in" these days, it is very often "garbage out". We need to retrieve our mind from the attic where it has often been stored. We need to let the Holy Spirit transform and recreate our wonderfully gifted mind.

I will make some modest suggestions for beginning to transform your mind. Read the four Gospels, especially concentrating on the Gospel of John. Read these along with a commentary, possibly by William Barclay, or read an expository book by Lloyd Ogilvie. Pick up a copy of a challenging book such as *Celebration of Discipline* by Richard Foster, or study a classic book on the person of Christ, like *The Life and Teachings of Jesus Christ* by James Stewart.

Each of us should have the goal of reading a book a month, perhaps concentrating on history, literature, poetry, theology, philosophy, or ethics. We have been given the gift of a magnificent mind; why not use it to prove what is *"good and acceptable and perfect."* Is your mind in shape, or is it just a bit flabby?

3. Wholeness of the Spirit

We are also called to develop our spirits. To find a sense of wholeness means to take seriously our body, our mind and our spirit. We need to expand and mature in the spiritual side of life. Handt Hanson, the Director of Worship and Music at Prince of Peace, has written a song which speaks to this need.

"In our worship we find new communion
In our worship our spirits join in union
In our worship our voices sing praise!
To the Father above for His wonderful love.

It's His spirit touching spirit that I love
It's His spirit touching spirit that changes my heart
When our spirits combine His love becomes mine
And His spirit can live in my heart."

It is so easy for us as Americans to neglect the spiritual side of life; we tend to be doers, not pray-ers or meditators. I attended a retreat a few years ago with a man who had spent the past 30 years as a contemplative priest. That meant the balance of his life had been spent in meditation and prayer. The rest of us in the group found this to be almost inconceivable. To think that someone could be so dedicated and committed to the development of the inner life, to the growth and maturity of the spirit! At the same time that most of us agreed that we did not believe we were called to this kind of monastic life personally, we also became aware of how little attention we give to the needs of the spirit.

The spiritual side of life has to do with the presence of God within, with our sense of awe, wonder and joy at the presence of Jesus Christ at the center of life. Handt Hanson has written another song which speaks to this sense:

"This is why we do the things we do for you
This is why we want to give you love
There is just one reason for this love we share
Listen closely, He's the one who brings us here.

It's Jesus in the center of my life you see
Jesus in the center of my life
It's very obvious to me, that's the reason I am free
It's Jesus in the center of my life."

It is easy to be unbalanced spiritually. So often study and action become more important than prayer and Bible study and personal faith. We can become experts in theology, in understanding and debating the issues, still never knowing what it means for God's Spirit to touch our spirit.

We develop the spiritual side of life in many different ways. It grows in worship, in the hearing of the Word of God, in the participation of the Sacraments. Some of the most beautiful and growing moments of our lives happen in the midst of worship, when some part of that experience impacts our life. It may be in the participation in the Sacrament; it may be during a musical selection; it may be during the prayer time; it may even be as someone comes and welcomes us to worship and is glad that we are present. Regular corporate worship is at the center of our spiritual growth.

Church is not the only place for spiritual growth; however, this also happens as we participate in regular Bible study, as the power and the life of the Scriptures touch us right where we are. There is nothing that can have the impact of immersing ourselves in the Gospel of John, or Philippians, 1 John, or the Psalms. To listen to what God is saying to us is a part of our spiritual growth and maturity.

Prayer is at the center of life in the Spirit. A great pianist talked about the need for constant practice. He said that if he misses practice one day, he begins to notice it. If he misses this work for two days, his family begins to notice it. And if he misses three days, then the audience begins to notice it. When we do not pray, when we are not in constant communication with God, then we notice it, our families notice it, and others can sense it.

I heard a good description about how one might pray. Take your hand and hold up the four fingers. The little finger reminds us to pray for those who are forgotten in this world — the neglected, the insignificant, the poor and oppressed. The fourth finger is the ring finger; this centers our prayer on those whom we love, those closest to us, our families and our friends. The middle finger reminds us to pray for the big people, those who are in leadership positions—government officials, community leaders, the people who have power and influence in our world. The second finger is the pointing finger; this reminds us to pray for those who point us to Christ—parents, pastors, Sunday school teachers, others who challenge us to live our faith. Then there is the thumb, pointing directly at us, reminding us to pray for ourselves that we might be the people God intends us to be.

Finally we develop our spirits by reading and absorbing some of the devotional literature that is available. Books by persons such as Henri Nouwen, Edna Hong, John Powell or Charles Allen come to mind. Devotional booklets are published by most denominations and have daily messages for each of us. As we touch the spirits of other Christians through these writings, we too can be more in touch with the spirit of Christ.

We need some goals for developing the spiritual side of life. We have been created in the image of God, and one of the dimensions of this creation is that we are spiritual beings. Are we growing in our spiritual walk? Do we have a sense of wholeness in our lives?

4. Wholeness of Emotions

Finally, there is the emotional side of our being, that which has to do with the feelings, the heart, the subjective part of us. Again, this is meant to be kept in a wholelistic balance with the rest of life. But very often there is a temptation to fall off the balance beam at this point. This imbalance seems more prevalent than any of the other types of wholeness. Two extremes of emotions seem to have emerged in the Christian community.

On the one hand, there are many Christians who say that emotions and subjective experience are at the center of the Christian life. Faith is described as being an emotional high. People act this out by throwing their hands into the air, speaking in tongues, shouting praise and alleluia throughout the day. Music, preaching and prayer are filled with emotion. Everything is kept at a rather high pitch.

On the other hand, many have reacted against the strong emotional tone described above, and have concluded that emotions are especially dangerous and best be avoided. They have declared that faith and worship have nothing at all to do with the heart, with the subjective part of us, with the emotive. Thus, we have often emphasized the objective nature of worship, of the Gospel, of Jesus Christ, and this sometimes has become emotionless. The sermons, music and liturgy are thus designed primarily to meet the needs of the mind. (Some which are very short are also meant to meet the needs of the body.)

I believe that the truth is found somewhere in-between these extremes. It is important to find a sense of balance, not falling off the balance beam on one side or the other. We certainly do not want only emotion in worship, getting people all worked up and turned on. We see our faith as being rooted and grounded in the person of Christ, not in some emotional high. An ecstatic experience may be some evidence of faith, but there is also faith to be found where there is not such emotion.

On the other hand, we need to affirm that there is an emotional side of our faith, and this should be present when the Christian community gathers for worship. When we sing the hymns, we often want to be stirred and lifted. When we hear the sermon for the day, we want this to impact our emotions as well as our minds. In a sense, we do want to be "strangely warmed" as the men on the road to Emmaus experienced when they were with Jesus.

In the prayer time on Sunday morning, we want to be emotionally touched by this event, speaking to God and also listening. Sometimes prayer can be very emotional. Recently we had a teenager in our community killed in a car accident, and the following Sunday scores of teenagers gathered at the altar rail during our time of prayer. Emotion was very much present. That's okay. As Christians we are able to cry as well as rejoice. We are encouraged to express our emotions, to embrace each other, to welcome each other. We do find that our faith does have something to do with the heart.

Wholeness should be our goal. We will never achieve complete wholeness because we are limited by our sinful nature. But we should be open to all four facets of our personhood. There is wholeness in body, in mind, in spirit, and in emotions. If we only develop one or two of these, we become like a weight lifter who may have huge arms and chest, but spindly legs, very much unbalanced. We want to find balance.

Thus as we begin to think about the reality of death, about being prepared, it is also best for us to think about a strong sense of balance in our lives right now. The entire wellness movement stresses the idea of being whole and healthy right now, so that life can be more abundant. The Bible says that we have been baptized into a living hope. We are not static beings, we do not have to remain the same. The Gospel offers us the chance to start over again, to find a wholeness we never experienced before, to be brand new people. *"If anyone is in Christ, he is a new creation, the old has passed away, behold the new has come" (2 Corinthians 5:17).*

If there is something in your life right now which is out of balance, if something destructive is dominating your body, spirit, mind or heart, then let Christ change you. Start over again, develop some new goals, make some new decisions about your life, find some new direction and friendships. Let the spirit breathe fresh air into what has so often become a rather stagnant and stale environment.

What is there today in you and me which makes us unhappy? Let's ask God to guide us as we work to change it. If the body is out-of-sorts, out-of-shape, overweight, sloppy, neglected, then change it. If the mind has gone to sleep, and you are addicted to the tube, then wake it up. If the spirit is empty and powerless, chasing after a rainbow that is not even there, then get moving in the right direction. If the emotions are playing tricks on you, if they are out of sorts more often than you would like, then find new ways to bring them into balance.

This is what it means to live a holy life, a beautiful life of wholeness and balance. Jesus said in words and actions, *"Behold I make all things new."* Body, mind, spirit, emotions brand new. *"The old has passed away, behold the new has come" (1 Corinthians 5:17).* This is the way God intended us to live. This is the best way to be prepared to die.

TWENTY QUESTIONS

*T*o reflect upon the meaning of the abundant life, to dwell on wholeness is rather exhilarating. It is tempting to stay right here and not move on to a discussion of the reality of death. However, this book's central purpose is to help us prepare for the inevitability of this life ending. We often do not like to think about this, but there comes a time when we can no longer avoid the issue. That time is now. This book is intended to help us think through all of the issues that surround us at the time of death, our death and the death of those who are close to us.

It should almost go without saying—but we need to say it anyway—that death comes to both the prepared and the unprepared. Death will come to each person. There are no exceptions. Death almost always comes before we want it to come. It is almost always a surprise, a shock, a devastating experience. It is far better to be prepared than to be unprepared. What does it mean to be prepared? To be ready means that a person has struggled with many different issues, and made a number of choices already that have been documented, communicated to loved ones, and agreed upon by the family members.

Sometimes I fear that we believe deep down in the center of our beings that if we do not think about death, if we do not mention it or plan for it, then it simply will not come. Out of sight, out of mind, out of the realm of possibility. We know this is not the case in our minds, but emotionally we live with this sense of denial, this unreality, believing that death just cannot happen to us. Many of us hold to the myth that if we wish intensely and persistently enough for the something *not* to happen, then it will not take place. It may sound silly when put in these terms, but this kind of thinking is most pervasive in our culture.

And so when death comes into the midst of our family — a grandparent, a parent, a brother or sister, a spouse, a child, a close friend — then we are very often rocked to the very center of our life. We just cannot believe it; it is so far beyond the realm of possibility that it cannot be true. We go to pieces, we are utterly devastated, because we truly believed that death happened only to others. Death is most assuredly a four-letter word in our society, perhaps the most obscene word in the vocabulary of typical Americans.

Christians often struggle with this whole phenomenon of death and dying. On the one hand, if there is anyone who should be ready to face death, it should be the person who has faith and trust in Jesus Christ. It is part of our basic belief system that death is not the last stanza in the hymn of life; there is something even better yet to come. We claim John 3:16 in a rather bold fashion, *"For God so loved the world that he gave his only begotten Son, that whosoever believes in him should not perish but have eternal life."*

Or we hold on tight to the words of the Apostle Paul, *"For me to live is Christ, but to die is gain" (Philippians 1:21)*. We know that if we live in Christ, we should not be afraid of death. We know that we should not find it so devastating and obscene. But the truth is that we do indeed view death as an enemy. We know we should have complete confidence in the promises of God, but somehow it is just not that easy. Most of us have done little or no planning for the day when we will no longer be on this earth. We haven't talked about death and the issues involved, thus we are basically unprepared.

There is a strong certainty present in the whole area of concern. If a family has not gone through any preparation for death, if there has been no discussion or planning when someone does die, it is that entire family who pays the price. If we have not made necessary plans and arrangements, then our family will suffer the consequences. I strongly emphasize the word "suffer". It is infinitely more difficult to go through a time of death when no advance preparation has taken place — when a family has no idea what the wishes of the deceased might be — than when there has been at least minimal planning and reasonable communication.

The purpose of this book is to declare with as much emphasis as possible, with as much urgency as can be engendered, that if you have not made prudent and final decisions regarding your own death, then you are basically saying to your family, "You take care of everything, I won't be here anyway." You are saying, "You take care of all the arrangements and details and hassles after I am gone, and by the way, I wish you my best." So often the family of one who dies ends up struggling with very complex, difficult issues and problems, many of them caused by a failure to plan ahead.

In some ways this seems strange, that we refuse to do the planning for what we know is coming. But it is a part of our American denial of death. We so often believe that death will probably come to us when we are 99 years old and by that time all of the decisions will be so easy they will not cause any problems to anyone. We can almost visualize how this will happen. As we approach that 100th birthday, as we look death in the face, then everyone will agree that death is now a blessing, and no one will be too surprised and saddened. It will be like stepping over the stream at the narrowest point. Unfortunately, this is not the way it usually happens.

This chapter will prepare a checklist, a guide for each person to use to assess his or her readiness for death. It would be most helpful if a family could discuss each of these 20 questions together and then come to some kind of common understanding. It would also be most helpful for pastors to talk about these questions in a sermon, so that congregations might begin to deal with these issues. Obviously the best time to do this work is now, when there is not the excruciating pain and emotion that are present at the time of death. But I say again, if we refuse to deal with this reality up-front, if we refuse to plan, then we are almost insuring a very difficult and painful time for all those who survive.

The 20 questions we all need to consider are as follows:

1. Do you have peace with God?

This is perhaps the most important question of all, and much of this book could be centered around considering the spiritual dimension of life and death. However, there seem to be many books in print today which confront this question in a most comprehensive way, but very few books which deal with the myriad of practical details that are present at the time of death. Thus I will concentrate on the latter, although suggesting strongly that the former is a crucial question for us all.

If you were to know that this was to be your last day on this earth, would you be ready to stand before our Lord? Is Jesus Christ the Lord and Savior of your life? Are you a part of a Christian community where you are growing and maturing in your faith and life? Are you following Christ as a servant in bringing love, hope and justice to this troubled world? Do you live for yourself or for others?

The most important truth revealed in the Scriptures, of course, is that we can never do enough to earn our way into the Kingdom of God, but that God in Christ has reached out to us in grace and love. People often look at the Christian life as being like a ladder which we climb on our pathway to God. However, as Martin Luther affirmed, there is no ladder. God reaches down to us; that is what amazing grace is all about. Paul writes in Ephesians 2:8, *"For by grace you have been saved through faith; and this is not your own doing, it is the gift of God."* Readiness involves our own acceptance of God's grace through Jesus Christ and our commitment to live in that gift.

I can legitimately ask the question, "If this was to be your last day on earth, would you be ready in terms of your spiritual journey?" It seems as if the proper readiness could be described by saying that you would not drastically change the way you lived on this last day from the way you normally live. It means that your values, your priorities, your relationships, and your goals are consistent with a Christian perspective. Therefore, the announcement that you have just one day to live would not change anything. To be ready means that God in Christ has made you his child in Baptism, and that he lives in you today. *"He who believes and is baptized shall be saved."* Are you ready?

2. Have you talked with members of your family about your death?

Has there been a spirit of openness about death, or a conspiracy of silence? Have you ever talked about the decisions that would need to be made when you die? As the life insurance salesperson says in all seriousness, "If something should happen to you . . ." Does your family know what your wishes might be, whom to call to make the arrangements, what choices would need to be made, where to find all the necessary documents, how much money would be available for the survivors? Have you ever talked with your family about the possibility and the reality of your own death? Or are you going to be the first person to somehow escape the experience of dying?

If you have not had such a discussion, if you have not sat around the kitchen table, in the living room or family room and talked about these matters of great urgency, then perhaps this book and chapter can help you begin to do what needs to be done. I would certainly encourage you to go through these questions in this chapter with your family, then come to some conclusions which can be written and communicated to all concerned. Don't put this off until the time is more convenient, or until someone gets older or faces some kind of serious illness. That moment may be too late.

3. Do you have a will?

Recently a study in America concluded that 71% of all people who died in a given year in the recent past did not have a will. That is astonishing and in many ways appalling. More than two-thirds of all the people who died did so without a will. It is hard to imagine the kind of pain, sorrow and agony this lack of preparation caused to the surviving families. It is also impossible to know how much money this took from the pockets of these families, but it no doubt was astronomical.

As we will discuss in more detail later on, it is not completely accurate to say that this 71% died without a will. Persons who die without creating wills of their own should be aware that the state in which they live has a will all made out for them. We must commend our government for being so thoughtful, to provide a written will for all those who are too busy or too uninformed to take care of such an action on their own.

I might also suggest that if we knew what was in that will of the government, if we knew all of the implications, we might not be completely enamored by its contents. But then you won't be around to worry about such mundane matters anyway; that will be left to those who survive. Be advised, however, that the government will decide, if you do not make out a will, who will receive your investments, your property, and even your children. This sounds like a marvelous deal. At the same time, if there is no will, a family might lose a tremendous percentage of the estate by way of taxes, just because of this failure to plan ahead. So the basic principle that should be considered is this: if you do not have a will, you are placing your family in much jeopardy. More information about a will is discussed later in this book.

4. If you have a will, has it been updated?

Congress changes the law often when it comes to our estate. For instance, in 1981 there were some substantial changes in the law, which may very well affect any will written before that date. In 1984 a few more minor changes were added to the tax code. As this book is being written, Congress is considering some further major changes in the tax code.

Thus, it is very important that you update the will on a regular basis, reflecting both the changes in federal and state law, as well as the changes that are constantly taking place in your own personal and family situation. This may sound only like a bonanza for attorneys, but failure to act can cost many times more than additional fees and can cause your family much consternation at the time of your death. It is always best to be completely aware and prepared.

5. If you have a will, does your family know where it is located?

Could your family members locate a copy of your will immediately if the need would suddenly arise? So often it seems as if our loved ones have no idea where a will is to be found, and this necessitates a frantic search at the time of death. There are enough surprises at this time without providing another surprise, such as a will that is lost. A story of Eva Jean in a later chapter will give a rather bizarre example of what can happen in such an instance.

There needs to be a record of all important documents, and where these might be found. This accounting should be given now to those closest to us. It is necessary that this information and the will not be kept in a safety deposit box. These are often sealed at the time of a death. However, there continues to be changes in the accessibility to these boxes, so it is best to know what the law might be in your area. Let your family know where all important papers are to be found. The forms in the back of this book should be helpful in this process.

6. Does your will reflect your values and priorities in life?

The will is referred to as the "last will and testament." Another way to say this is to call the will the last testimony, the last chance to give a statement of one's faith, life and beliefs. What does your will say about what was most important to you? Does it say anything about your Christian convictions, about what is truly important to you? The will should reflect the same values in death that were present and pre-eminent in life.

Thus, if it was important in life for you to give to others, to be a generous steward of God's resources, then this is what should be reflected in the will. As we have given sacrificially in life, so we can also give in death. This can be to our local congregation, to church colleges, to seminaries, to world hunger, to the cancer society, to a multitude of worthwhile charitable organizations. Giving at the time of death can be a tremendously important part of our estate planning.

For those who have larger estates, much more can be given away than we could ever imagine. This will be discussed in more detail later in the book, but there are some highly creative ways which are available as we seek to give. Government tax policies have been created over the past decades in order to encourage such giving to charity, and so we should be aware of all the implications of such giving.

In addition, there is also the question of passing wealth to our heirs. Certainly we would wish for our spouse and children to receive generous amounts of resources for their own continued living and comfort. This should go without saying. But at the same time, there is certainly a question in the minds of many whether those with substantial assets should leave all of these resources to their children and grandchildren. Is it good for these heirs to be given everything, to be wealthy before they have been able to earn anything for themselves? This seems like a broken record in our society, that many heirs who have been given so much have not measured up to the expectations of those originally earning the wealth. Does inherited wealth motivate our children, or does it prove to be more harmful in the long run? I am not making judgments about this, as it remains for each family to make these decisions. But it seems that those who have substantial holdings should consider strongly giving some of that away at the time of death, rather than just passing it all down to the survivors. Now is the time to discuss these issues and see what is possible under the present tax and estate policies of the government.

7. Do you have a guardian for your children?

For those who have dependent children, this may be the most important decision of all. At this point, the need for someone in a guardianship capacity may seem a very remote possibility, but there are many examples in our world where this has been a tragic necessity. A guardian should be a person or persons who can give to your children the kind of love, the kind of values, the kind of faith, the kind of opportunities that you would have desired for them.

Oftentimes a sponsor at the baptism of a child is also designated as a guardian. However, there is no automatic connection at this point, sponsorship does not entail guardianship. This is a special designation in a person's will that will make provision for the children if the parents are no longer present. For the sake of the children, this decision should be made carefully, prayerfully and immediately, if it has not already been decided.

8. Have you named an executor for your will?

An executor is a person who will serve as your personal representative in all legal and financial matters in the case of your death. This person will be responsible for paying all of your final expenses, for collecting all of your assets, and for preparing the estate for the courts. You will obviously want a person in this position who will be your advocate, who will make sure that all of your wishes are implemented. Of course, it would be very helpful if you would tell this person what these wishes are while you are still alive and also document them in writing. This is no time to take any chances; you need to name the right person, one in whom you have a high degree of trust and confidence, and you need to write down what you want to be done.

9. Are all of your important papers in a place where they can be found easily?

There is nothing as frustrating for a grieving family than to have to undergo a search of the house to try and find the important papers at the time of death. This creates far more anxiety than is necessary. Thus, it is best that all documents be in a place which is clearly marked and known to the members of your family. The specific papers which are necessary are highlighted in the forms at the back of this book.

It is important to have more than one copy of these papers. The original should be present in the home, and a copy should be located somewhere else. This could be in the safety deposit box. This is not a time to play "I've Got a Secret" with your family.

10. Do you have anything in the safety deposit box which will be needed at the time of death?

As mentioned earlier, it is best to have the copies of papers needed at the time of death located somewhere else. There is a change going on in the law. In the state of Minnesota, for instance, a surviving spouse can gain entry to this box after a death. However, this does not apply to other members of the family. Understand and take into account the laws of the state in which you live, so that you do not have to confront a sealed safety deposit box containing essential papers.

11. Have you decided about organ donation?

More information on organ donation is contained later in this book in Chapter Seven. Such decisions should appropriately be made long before a death occurs. Some states have made this decision especially convenient by enabling you to indicate this on your driver's license. However, this is a family decision, and it is not at all fair to force a family to make this decision at the time of death. At the time of shock and dismay, there is often just too much pain present for a family to respond in a way that might have been possible at an earlier time.

12. Do you wish an earth burial or cremation?

In past generations, this was not a decision which faced most Americans or most Christians, but now with the rapid growth in the number of cremations, and the rapidly accelerating costs of cemetery burials, cremation has become an alternative for many. From a theological point of view, there is no valid reason why cremation should not be considered; this will depend solely on the feelings and convictions and traditions of the family. Once again, it is far easier to face this issue long before a death has taken place. More information is found later in this book in Chapter Nine.

13. If you wish an earth burial, where do you desire that this take place?

Many people who live in more rural areas, or who belong to a church which has its own cemetery, will find this to be a non-issue. But for most persons living in urban areas, this is indeed a most important consideration. There are a number of alternatives that are possible. It is good to know that generally the cost of burial plots in more rural areas is considerably less than the cost in urban or suburban communities.

To state this issue in more dramatic terms, I do not believe that it is fair for a family to have to make the decision of the place of burial in just an hour or two, shortly after a death. However, that is exactly what happens when people do not deal with this issue ahead of time. It would be far better if a family which is alive and well would take a drive around several cemeteries in the area, check the respective prices and other information, and then choose a place acceptable to the family. It is far better to do this now.

14. Which funeral home, if any, do you wish to handle the arrangements at the time of death?

If you wish to utilize a funeral home, have you made that decision? For those living in smaller communities, there may not be an alternative, but those living in more urban areas face numerous choices. Some of these decisions will be dictated by whether there is cremation or burial, as well as by the traditions and religious beliefs of the family. Hopefully, something about the cost of the funeral arrangements will have been examined before an actual death takes place.

It would be most helpful if you would visit some funeral homes in the area in order to create more awareness and understanding of this whole process. You should ask about prices and the various alternatives that would be available to you. It is not nearly as difficult to make some decisions when the health is good and the sun is shining.

15. Where do you wish for your funeral or memorial service to be held?

I believe it is best for Christians to have this service in that place where so many of their life-changing experiences have taken place, the church, but times and circumstances may dictate that the service should be held elsewhere. More information is given later.

16. How much money do you wish your family to spend on your funeral?

Most people do not have the vaguest notion of how high funeral costs can be in this time of history. We may not have been in the market for a funeral for a long time, if ever, and we may experience what the automobile industry refers to as "sticker shock". When we see the costs of the casket and other goods and services, we might be overwhelmed.

Thus, it is important that we determine with our family how

much should be spent on our funeral, and just as crucial, the source of the money. Often a family spends money that it does not have, and that is not good stewardship or planning. Most often, if a family has limited financial resources, it would be far better to use as much as is possible for the living rather than spending more than is needed on arrangements for the dead. Talking about these issues ahead of time can prevent unnecessary feelings of guilt or anger from surfacing later.

The average cost of a funeral in 1987 can be anywhere from $4,000 to $6,000, and many will cost much more. It is appropriate for a family to spend substantial dollars on a funeral, if this has been agreed upon in advance and there are the necessary financial resources available. It is not appropriate for a family to spend out of pressure or haste, when there are not sufficient monies to do so. In addition, it is also appropriate to spend very little money on a funeral, to pursue a low-cost alternative. However, this depends on the feelings and planning of the individual family. It is best to discuss and plan this now.

17. Does your family have a listing of all the death benefits which are available to them?

Every family situation is unique, and there can be benefits that comes from a wide variety of sources. Insurance, Social Security, veteran's benefits, and company pensions are just a few that need to be considered and investigated. Complete statements of all benefits and assets for the survivors would be invaluable at the time of death. These again should be stored in a place where they can be easily located.

18. Does your family know where your safety deposit box is located (If you have one) and where you have placed both keys?

It is not unusual for a family to be completely unaware of the presence of a safety deposit box. It is even more common for a family to have no idea where the keys might be kept, and thus have much difficulty gaining access. There are usually two keys for such a box, and they should not be located in the same place.

Again this is a simple precaution, but if ignored, can cause much consternation.

19. Do you have copies of your birth certificate, and where applicable, your marriage certificate?

These documents will be needed at the time of a death to claim some of the benefits. Often a spouse or family does not know where to even call or write for this information. It is best that we have all of the necessary certificates for each member of our family well ahead of any need for them, and that there is a clear understanding of where these are to be found.

20. If you and / or your spouse are veterans, do you have the discharge papers?

In order to be buried at a national cemetery, or to claim the deserved benefis, a copy of these papers must be presented. I have seen too many instances where a family has had no idea where these papers are to be found. When a death has just occurred, it is not the best time to start a search.

In summary, there are more questions that could be asked, but these are among the most important. In my own experience of being with families at times of death, most have not answered the majority of the questions listed above. They have had many good intentions of doing something, they have talked around some of the issues, but the actual work and effort has not been done. Thus, a time of real confusion and pain is created. A few hours taken in preparation ahead of time could have saved weeks, months and years of frustration and unneeded bitterness.

The purpose of this book, however, is not to just ask the questions and then let it be. The remainder of the chapters will attempt to answer the questions that were asked, and to give information and help for those seeking to plan. Are you ready for death? There are no guarantees, but once you have fully answered all of the 20 questions of this chapter, you will be much more prepared than you may be now. That is the goal I pursue.

A STORY
OF DEATH

*T*he phone rang late one January afternoon. It was a call from a man I had never met, but he was a fellow worker for a many from our congregation. He called to tell me that Phil had suffered what appeared to have been a very serious heart attack, he had collapsed at work and had been rushed to a nearby hospital. Phil's wife Audrey and son Scott had been contacted, and they were now on the way to be with him. I told the caller that I would immediately head out to the hospital.

It struck me as I hurried to the car how shocked and stunned I was by this news. As a pastor I am less surprised by events and circumstances than I used to be. In a larger congregation it seems that a certain percentage of the membership is in one kind of a crisis or another at all times, so I am constantly confronted with pain, sickness and heartache.

However, Phil was only 47 years old and by all outward appearances, in excellent health. I just had difficulty comprehending that anything serious could happen to him. He was always vigorous, a president of our congregation some years earlier, an avid skier. He just looked healthy. But now word had come that he was very ill. I prayed as I drove, for Phil and Audrey, for son Scott and his new bride Julie, and for daughter Ann away at college. I now remember very little about the drive to the hospital.

When I arrived at the emergency room, Audrey and Scott were already there, waiting in a room just adjacent to where the medical team was at work on Phil. We quickly embraced, and tears were abundant. It was obvious that both of them were in a state of shock. Everything about this event and location was so unreal, so unbelievable as to be almost beyond comprehension. We prayed together for Phil, and pleaded desperately for his health and life.

A doctor came to see us and gave us some preliminary findings. At this time there was nothing more to report; they had taken tests and these were not completed as of yet. He assured us that Phil was receiving excellent and immediate care, everything was being done for him which could be done. The somber demeanor of the doctor gave rise to all of our deep-seated fears. We kept praying for the difficult moment.

Audrey and Scott talked about the events of the day, how everything had seemed so normal and ordinary until the phone call came just a few minutes before. Phil left for work that morning just as he always had; there did not seem to be anything different about him or the day. At the same time though, he had been under much strain at work in recent weeks, and Audrey admitted she had been very worried about him. We made a few phone calls to close relatives and friends. Some of them offered to come immediately to the hospital.

The time of waiting seemed to be endless. Each time a friend or relatives would arrive, Audrey and Scott would go through a new period of emotional release, embracing those who came, and sharing together the grief and pain and shock. Scott's wife Julie joined us and became a part of those who waited. Not knowing what had happened and what was being done at the time was as painful and difficult, or even more so, than any other part of the experience.

Finally, a doctor came in with a bitterly grim report. The tests had demonstrated that this had not been a heart attack at all, but rather a massive cerebral hemorrhage. There had been a good deal of bleeding in the brain, and the prognosis was not good. There was a strong chance that brain damage had already occurred, and there was a question as to whether he would survive the next few hours. The news could hardly have been worse.

Again we shared tears and prayers and held each other as we waited. Some of the awful reality was then beginning to sink in to each of us as we waited in that family room. The doctor took me aside as the pastor and told me that he was very glad I was there, for in the next few hours there would be some very difficult decisions that would need attention. He also shared with me that he did not think Phil was going to make it.

Scott and Audrey spent some of the time calling those who should know what was happening; this act of calling was therapeutic and calming. In a time of utter helplessness, it is often good to have something that grieving people can do, to help them feel they are doing something positive and necessary. Phone calls can help. Several calls were made to daughter Ann, arranging for a way to bring her home by the next morning. Audrey found more than a little solace in being a comfort to her children and daughter-in-law. I tried to stay close to them, getting them to take walks in the corridor, to move around a bit, to have at least a minimal amount to eat.

It is instructive to see the dramatic change that has happened in hospitals in recent years. In the past, it was often impossible to know what was actually taking place. There was a cloak of secrecy and silence that was pervasive. But it seems as if the pendulum has swung to the other direction, and now the medical personnel usually lay all of the cards on the table, often holding nothing back. The doctors now are often graphically honest.

This is certainly preferable to the old way of doing things, but sometimes the medical personnel in their desire to be truthful seem to demonstrate a decided lack of compassion or an understanding of the family's grief and sorrow. Thus, I found that a pastor can often be an interpreter, a mediator, helping the family understand more clearly what has been said by the doctors and nurses. At the same time the pastor can help the medical staff understand and appreciate the feelings of the family.

Late that evening the doctor came to say that Phil was stable, but that he was breathing only with the aid of a machine. However, no final decisions would be made about removing life support systems that evening; these decisons would wait until the next day. Thus, some of us decided that it would be best to go home and get some rest; there was nothing more to be done that evening. Audrey, Scott, Julie, and a couple of other family members remained at the hospital, promising to sleep as much as possible. We knew that sleep would be difficult at best, but we encouraged them to take care of their own health. They could not be of much help to anyone if they became sick.

Early the next morning we returned to the hospital to begin the painful vigil again. The hospital was going to do some tests. If there was no brain response, they would wait several hours to do the same tests a second time. At that time, if the results were the same, they would turn off the machines. What terribly painful and wrenching hours these were. Ann arrived from college. Again it was a time of deep anguish for all of us, trying to help her as she experienced the intensity of grief. Friends and family continued to stop by, some of them bringing comfort, some needing comfort.

As the time for the final tests came closer, the hospital staff talked to me about the possibility of organ donation. I hardly knew how to broach the subject; there had already been almost more suffering than one family could bear. To talk about organ donation at a time like this seemed to be so cold and morbid. Yet it had to be done. Audrey and Phil had not made any decision about this ahead of time, so Audrey had no clear understanding of what would be best.

Finally, later in the afternoon, almost 24 hours after we had been called to the hospital, several of us stood by Phil's bedside as the life support systems were turned off. The nurse in charge was extremely helpful and sensitive, and this made it easier for us all. As we stood there we had a sense of both peace and sorrow, and we gave a prayer of thanks for Phil's life. We also expressed confidence that there would come a day when we would see Phil again. Then we went out to tell the rest of the family members that it was over.

But many things were not over. The time of decision-making had arrived in dramatic fashion. The hospital wanted to know whether the family wanted an autopsy, which would attempt to discover exactly what had happened to Phil and would also assist the medical profession in its ongoing search for medical knowledge. Again this was a difficult decision, and we spent many minutes talking it through.

Next we had needed to discuss which funeral home to contact. I gave them the names of several homes in our area, and they chose one not far from their home. We talked about the time of the funeral. Because there were so many elderly persons who would be coming from out of town, it was thought best to hold the funeral during the late morning, so people could return home before sunset. We talked about the location of the funeral service. There was no question; it would be held at the church where Phil and Audrey had deep roots.

Other decisions needed to be considered. What about a memorial fund? It was decided to establish one at the church, but the actual designation of these funds could happen at a later date. How about a burial? Phil was a veteran so the national cemetery located nearby was chosen. I wished at that time that we had a brochure containing all of the information and options, but it was something we just had not done at our church. (Later on Scott, Julie and I would work with others at our church to create such a brochure — a copy is available from Prince of Peace Lutheran Church, 13801 Fairview Drive, Burnsville, Minnesota 55337.)

The next day the family went to the funeral home to make the necessary arrangements, taking with them some family friends to help make these difficult decisions. Later that day I spent time with Audrey, Scott, Julie and Ann in planning for the funeral service. Scott chose a high school teacher of his to sing at the service, and a close friend of Phil and Audrey's was asked to give a greeting from the family, a eulogy.

The members of our congregation also became involved. Much food was brought to the home, and people offered to help in a multitude of ways. Others prepared a dinner that could be served to the family and other mourners after the funeral service was complete. Many expressions of love, support and prayer flowed out from people. They came to the home almost nonstop during the first days following Phil's death.

On the night before the funeral service, there was a time of visitation at the local funeral home. In many ways this was a comforting occasion. Large numbers of people came, embracing Audrey, Scott, Julie and Ann, sharing love and sorrow. I am always amazed at how thoughtful and caring people can be when Christ lives in them, and there was certainly much evidence of that spirit at the time of visitation.

The day of the funeral was clear and cold, with a bitter northwest wind. The temperature was below zero. But the church was warmed by the sunshine and the huge crowd of people present. There was even a busload of people from the business where Phil was employed. Because of the weather, we suggested that many of the elderly not journey with us to the cemetery, but remain for coffee until the rest of the group would return.

The funeral service began with our singing the hymn "Beautiful Savior", followed by Scripture readings from Psalm 23, John 14:1-6, and Romans 8:31-39. All of these had been chosen by the family. We had solos of "Amazing Grace" and "How Great Thou Art", sung in stirring and dramatic fashion. One family friend gave an inspired and personal greeting on behalf of the family. We sang "Children of the Heavenly Father" and "O God, Our Help in Ages Past".

The meditation was meant to proclaim the Gospel of Jesus Christ in as strong a way as possible, and also to somehow reflect the pain and anguish that were present. The following are the words of my funeral sermon:

Just a little past four o'clock last Thursday we received the message that Phil had been taken to the emergency unit of Hennepin County General Hospital. The first word that came was that he had suffered a heart attack.

When I arrived at the hospital about five, Scott and Audrey were talking to the hospital staff, but it was too early to tell what had happened. We prayed, we wept, we desperately pleaded for good news once the tests were completed.

The time of waiting was almost unbearable. Soon the doctors came and told us that Phil had suffered an aneurysm in the area of the brain, and it was very serious. From that time the reports just kept getting worse until finally, the next afternoon, Phil died. Just 24 hours after entering the hospital, Phil was no longer with us.

And all we could do was to cry out, what a tragedy! How we wanted him to live, to share his life and love with us 30 or 40 more years. All that was within us called out that this just could not be, we could not let him go, much of life was just beginning. Scott and Julie were recently married, Ann is completing college. Life was just beginning, not ending. And none of us could understand why.

Still this morning, the events of last Thursday and Friday are almost too much for any of us to comprehend. Phil went off to work in the morning as he always did and kissed Audrey goodbye. There seemed to be nothing unusual or different about that day. Phil had been under much stress at work, but stress is a part of all work and life, and there were few, if any indications that Phil's health was in danger.

So we are here today with many questions and very few answers. Words seem to fail us. We would like some rational explanation for why these things happen, why death takes a man like Phil in the prime of life, but we don't know why and probably never will on this earth. All we are able to say today is that we are still in shock, that we will greatly miss him, and that we cannot imagine life without him.

However, I would like to try and say a couple of words that might give us some sense of perspective. Any words will be terribly inadequate, but let me suggest three things that we might ponder.

First, I would encourage all of us here not to let Phil's tragic and premature death overshadow his life. It would be so easy today to just concentrate on his death, rather than to be moved by and inspired by his life. But we all know that it is in life that he impacted each of us; it is in life that he gave us so much.

So today, remember Phil's life. Remember that he was above all a child of God, baptized into the life and death and resurrection of Jesus Christ. Remember that he was raised in a Christian home and always lived close to the center of the Christian community and church.

Remember that he confirmed his faith as a teenager, that he assisted in the chaplaincy while in the military, and that, as a charter member of this congregation, he served as our president in those early years. Just 20 years ago this month our congregation was organized, and Phil and Audrey have been an integral part ever since.

This past Saturday we celebrated the Sacrament of Holy Communion, and I was very glad to see kneeling at the altar rail Phil and Scott, Audrey and Ann, receiving Christ once again into the center of their lives. We remember Phil's life and his faith, and we give thanks for his witness in our midst.

We also remember his devotion to his family, to Audrey, to Scott, to Ann, and now to Julie, to his mother and sisters and brothers. He was so proud that Scott had moved back to this area, that he and Julie were married. He was so proud of Ann and her accomplishments in college. Many of you have told me that Phil was very much like his father, with a rock-like faith and a compassionate heart. So today, let's remember his life. What he has given to us can never be taken away.

A second word. To all of the members of Phil's family, be assured today that you are not alone. You are surrounded by the people of God, the caring Christian community, and it is at a time like this that we see most clearly the tremendous power and love of the Christian church.

When we share our burdens with another, those burdens are not quite as heavy. When we walk with another's arms around us, it is not quite so difficult to walk. And I know that Phil's family has seen so much evidence of this caring, hundreds of people reaching out to hold them up, to remember, to weep together, to share the pain.

This past Sunday several different congregations stopped to remember you in prayer. All weekend so many have called or stopped by to express love. At the funeral home last evening there were hundreds who came to share hope and support. Again today, all of these friends and loved ones assure you that you are not alone.

God has chosen to work through people, people just like us, and God makes it possible for us to bear even a tragedy like this, by holding close to each other. To you, Audrey, Ann, Scott, Julie, and all the rest, you have been so kind and gracious to so many others who have gone through heartache. Now you are receiving this love in return.

We want you to know that we love you and we weep with you, and we will walk with you through this hour and the difficult times to come. Remember that you are never alone.

A third word. When we were standing in the intensive care unit next to Phil's bed, Scott walked over to the window. He motioned for me to come over and join him. He had something he was looking at that he also wanted me to see. I thought he was going to point to the Metrodome; I could see it dominating much of the skyline of downtown Minneapolis.

But instead he pointed across the street to the First Covenant Church, and the lighted cross on the top of that beautiful edifice. "That cross," he said, "that cross is the only hope we have. That is the only thing right now that makes any sense at all."

Today we realize again that no matter how much technology we have in our world, no matter how sophisticated we think we might be, no matter how wealthy as a nation we may have become, when it comes to the time of death, we realize how helpless we are. Computers may transform our world, but not even a computer can save us.

For that we need a Savior. And the whole Christmas message comes pouring in upon us, *"For to you is born this day in the city of David, a Savior, who is Christ the Lord."* This is all we have, and it is all we need.

The whole meaning of the Gospel is that death is not the end but rather a new beginning. All of the Scriptures talk about a time of reunion, when we shall see each other again, when there will be a new heaven and a new earth. Listen again to some of the most magnificent promises we have been given:

Psalm 23
"Even though I walk through the valley of the shadow of death, I will fear no evil, for thou art with me. Surely goodness

and mercy shall follow me all the days of my life and I shall dwell in the house of the Lord forever."

Revelation 21

"I saw a new heaven and a new earth, and I heard a great voice from the throne saying, 'Behold the dwelling of God is with men. He will dwell with them and they shall be his people, and God himself will be with them, he will wipe away every tear from their eyes and death shall be no more, neither shall there be mourning or crying nor pain any more, for the former things have passed away.'"

John 14

"Peace I leave with you, my peace I give to you, not as the world gives do I give to you. Let not your hearts be troubled, neither let them be afraid."

John 16

"So you have sorrow now, but I will see you again and your hearts will rejoice and no one will ever take your joy from you."

And then the majestic words of Romans 8:38-39, *"For I am absolutely convinced that neither death nor life, nor angels nor principalities, nor things present nor things to come, nor height, nor depth, nor anything else in all creation, will be able to separate us from the love of God in Christ Jesus."*

Today is a day of crushing pain. But I cannot imagine how much more painful it would be without the hope we have in Jesus Christ. We can lift our eyes from the casket and see the cross.

Remember Jesus' words, *"I will come again and I will take you to myself, so that where I am you will be also." "My hope is built on nothing less, than Jesus' blood and righteousness." "For me to live is Christ and to die is gain."* Let the promises be in us and over us for as long as we shall live.

I would like to close with the words of one of the great hymns of the church, "O God, Our Help in Ages Past". Turn to this hymn in your hymnbooks, and we will sing this hymn at the conclusion of the service.

O God, our help in ages past,
Our hope for years to come.
Our shelter from the stormy blast,
And our eternal home.

Under the shadow of your throne,
Your saints have dwelt secure.
Sufficient is your arm alone,
And our defense is sure.

Before the hills in order stood,
Or earth received its frame.
From everlasting you are God,
To endless years the same.

A thousand ages in your sight,
Are like an evening gone,
Short as the watch that ends the night,
Before the rising sun.

Time, like an ever rolling stream,
Soon bears us all away,
We fly forgotten, as a dream,
Dies at the opening day.

O God, our help in ages past,
Our hope for years to come.
Still be our guard while troubles last,
And our eternal home.

When the funeral service was over, we traveled that sad and sorrowful road to the cemetery. It was bitterly cold that day, which just seemed to accentuate the coldness and bleakness that many of us felt. At the same time there was a brilliant sun shining on the whiteness of the snow, giving evidence of a light that was brighter than any darkness. We gathered at the graveside for a very brief committal service. Following these goodbyes, we then returned to the church for a time of lunch and greeting of the family. The time of the reception was a very good time, a healing time, an outpouring of support and love.

The funeral was over, but most of the grief work was just beginning. Friends and family quickly return to their everyday lives and concerns after a funeral, but those most closely affected by a death can never go back to life as usual. For Audrey, Scott, Julie and Ann, there were many persons who were there for them when needed. That is a tremendous comfort and help at the time of death. There is no way to underestimate the power of such a caring community. But at the same time, as the weeks and months go by, grief sometimes becomes harder and more pronounced than at the beginning.

I tried to visit Audrey on a weekly basis for the first month or two, sometimes by a personal visit in the home, sometimes on the phone, and on occasion in my office. Scott and I also talked several times, trying to sort out what had taken place and what he should now be doing as the only remaining male in the family. Ann went back to college, so personal contact was not possible with her except when she returned home on break.

There were many painful firsts for them all: birthdays, Easter, Christmas, other special holidays. Every one of these days brought home more graphically the reality of the situation, that Phil would no longer be a part of these celebrations. At the same time, though, this family lived with a spirit of thankfulness for all of the years that he had been present, and they looked forward to a new day when there would be a reunion. More than a year after Phil's death, the grieving process is not completely over; it just takes a lot of time to move through. And that is okay. Deep and close relationships which are lost take a great deal of time to work through, as does beginning to start over again in a new way.

In summary, it is obvious that not every death happens like the one described above. There are as many variations on this theme as there are people. But there are some common experiences that are present in most death situations, and this chapter may be helpful by detailing some of the progression and emphasis of these events. It also gives an introduction to what the role of the pastor might be in the event of a death, again allowing for all of the differences that might be present in the situation. However, it does set the stage for the work and ministry of the pastor, which is the subject of the next chapter.

ROLE OF
THE PASTOR

*A*t the time of death, a parish pastor can be among the most valuable and integral sources of help and support for a grieving family. Here is where the Christian pastor is able to bring to bear all of the training, faith and empathetic skills that are hopefully a part of his or her ministry. In addition, this is also where a pastor often "succeeds" or "fails" in the ministry. For in the midst of a crisis, especially as this relates to a death, people expect that a pastor will be there for them, giving considerable love, care and hope. Therefore, I believe that there is no more important part of the parish ministry than to be present and involved in the whole experience of death, as well as in the resulting grief process. The pastor should be a vital and significant resource at the time of death.

Sometimes however, almost too much responsibility is put on the shoulders of the pastor. Many people often see the value and meaning of the funeral as being based almost exclusively on what has been done or said by the pastor, or on what has not been said or done. If the pastor has demonstrated strong sensitivity and empathy, both in personal encounters with the bereaved and in the public leadership of the funeral service, the people will usually see the experience as full of validity and purpose. If, on the other hand, the pastor shows a decided lack of understanding and caring, then the whole experience is judged to be less than it should or could have been. No pastor should ever underestimate the importance and impact of his or her ministry and message at the time of a death.

I will spend the remainder of this chapter highlighting the role of the pastor when that call comes concerning a death in the parish, or in the community. This role may take on many different dimensions, depending upon the specific circumstances, as well as the prior relationship the pastor has had with the deceased and the family. The extent of the pastor's involvement also will depend a good deal on whether this was a sudden, unexpected death, or whether the deceased has been dying over an extended period of time. But no matter what the special dynamics might be, there are some basics which should be present, as well as a solid commitment from the pastor to do all that is possible, to be a source of comfort and help.

I will suggest 12 guidelines for the pastor who is called to give competent and professional leadership concerning death:

1. The pastor should prepare the congregation for the reality of death and grief.

We often do not think much about this point, but actually what is done ahead of time, what is suggested in advance can be as helpful as anything else which is done at the time of death. Good preparation of a congregation for the reality of death is extremely important and effective. The pastor should talk about death from the pulpit, dealing with the pain and promise in a straightforward way, as well as with some of the realities that accompany death. The pastor should consider teaching classes and seminars in the area of death and dying, helping people to wrestle with the real issues that confront us on this earth. The pastor might also help the congregation put together a brochure containing some basic information about death. Hopefully, such a publication would be a valuable resource when death comes.

To encourage members of the congregation to prepare for the event of their own death is especially important. Each person should be given an opportunity to complete the forms that are presented in the back portion of this book, and to make some basic decisions ahead of time. The pastor needs to challenge members of the church to be ready for death, both in terms of a relationship with God, and also in terms of relationships with one another. It is so easy to deny or ignore the reality of death until it actually occurs. Good preparation can be the building block for good grief.

2. Where there is a terminal illness, the pastor should be very close to the dying person and family.

There are many times when a pastor will have an opportunity to minister to someone who is in failing health, who is not given very long to live. While this can be a very painful and wrenching time for all concerned, it also provides unique openings for the pastor to share some of the deepest and most profound ministry possible. Much of the time our conversation with each other tends to be superficial; we talk about the weather, sports and the economy. But when someone is staring death in the face, the time for dancing all around the fringes of the ultimates in life is definitely over. This is the right time for sharing the basic resources of our Christian faith, the Word of God, the Sacrament of Holy Communion, the comforting prayer.

A Roman Catholic priest friend of mine introduced me to a wonderful idea, what he called the "home mass". When he ministers to a family where one of the members is afflicted with a terminal illness, he will often suggest that the family gather together for a time of celebration. This family meal and reunion most often takes place in the home of the family, although the hospital could be an alternative if there is no other choice. But at the celebration the family honors the person who is ill. There is plenty of time for members of the family to tell this special guest how much he or she has meant to them over the years. It is a time to recall humorous as well as serious memories, and to give thanks as a family together for all of the blessings. It is a time of laughter, closeness and tears. And it is a good time.

Then the priest shares the Sacrament of the Holy Communion with the family, beginning with the guest of honor and then offering the bread of life to all of the others. The guest might even take part in the administration of the Sacrament, depending on the specific condition of this person and his / her religious tradition. In my own experience, this has been a moving time for a family, and I would strongly recommend this idea to others. So often a family joins together at the time of a funeral and spends many hours remembering those special memories of the past, laughing and crying together. Why not do this when the loved one is still alive and is able to enjoy such a beautiful and precious time of closeness and love?

One practical problem always seems to surface when we deal with terminal illness. Often the person will not actually admit that death is near. I have had the experience on many occasions of the ill person telling me, "Death is not very far away, but don't tell this to my family." I also talk to the family, and they share the concerns of the imminent death, of which they are well aware, but then they tell me that I should not tell the sick person the gravity of the situation. I often wonder, who is kidding who, why play these charades? What is happening is that people are missing out on sharing some of the most moving and meaningful times in all of life. When people deny the reality of death, it is very difficult for them to truly support each other.

Hopefully, the pastor will be able to bring about some of the needed dialogue and the acceptance of reality, so that the healing and grieving process might be facilitated. Again, much of this will depend on the specific circumstances, as well as on how the pastor relates to the family and their needs.

3. The pastor should go immediately when informed of a death.

This is often a moot issue, for the pastor in many situations is already with the family at the time of death. This becomes a pivotal time for ministry. If this is not the case, however, and a call comes to the pastor, whether it be night or day, it is essential that the pastor go to the family without delay. Often the person who calls will say that it is not necessary to come to the home or the hospital at that time, but I have found over the years that it is almost always best to go. This is really what the family wants. People do not want to infringe on the pastor's time, but in calling the pastor they are indicating a need for ministry. So many uncertainties, emotional upheavals and fears emerge at the time of death, that the presence of a pastor is often very necessary.

The first response of the pastor when arriving at the place where the family is gathered is simply to be there to listen, to empathize, to love. What is said is not so important; to share how sorry and sad he or she feels *is* important. This is a time for hugging, holding and listening. There may come a time in the grief work to give some profound theological statements, but not during this first contact. Rather, this is a time for quiet conversation and touching. A time of prayer is often appropriate, depending on the situation and the setting, but it should be brief and sensitive to the feelings which are present.

4. The pastor can help to make the first important decisions.

Very often during strong emotional crisis, a family has no idea what needs to be done or where to begin. A pastor can help in a gentle way to assist the family in starting to confront the necessary decisions. More information about the decisions to be made is found in Chapter Seven, and this information deals specifically with the immediate plans for the disposition of the body and for the setting of an appropriate time for the funeral. Specific details, such as the exact nature of the funeral service, should be left for a later time. It is enough in this initial stage to just make the most important overall decisions. The pastor can also help the family determine who should be contacted. For the most part, it is best that the bereaved do most of the calling, as it is part of the grief process; it gives them the opportunity to receive much support and love from those they contact.

During the time of these first decisions the pastor can assess the support system which is present for the grieving family. If there are plenty of friends and family who are providing care and comfort and strength, then the pastor can be quite confident that the initial emotional needs of the family will be met. If, on the other hand, the bereaved family is pretty much alone, without significant human support, then the pastor should find a group of people within the congregation who might bring needed love and empathy to the family. This could be neighbors and friends who have already demonstrated a degree of compassion, or it could be members of the church who have been trained in some form of caring ministry. Programs like the Stephen Ministry and Befrienders are examples of such training efforts. Very often a family will have a strong network of support available, but if not, the pastor needs to take some leadership in developing such a network.

5. The pastor should offer to go with the family to the funeral home.

The visit to the funeral home is often among the most traumatic events that accompany a death in the family. The pastor should be available to help if needed. This again will depend on a number of factors, but this offer is one which a grieving family usually appreciates. It is very helpful for people in grief to have someone with them who has been through this kind of experience, someone who has an understanding of the decisions which need to be made, and of the implications of those decisions.

Funeral directors often are ambiguous about the presence of the pastor at the funeral home. Some will appreciate the support and caring that a pastor might bring; others will be defensive out of fear that the pastor might encourage the purchase of a less expensive funeral. However, our response to the needs of the grieving family should never be determined by the attitude of the funeral director. Our first responsibility is to provide a ministry of comfort, help and encouragement to those who have suffered such a grievous loss.

At the funeral home, it is never the responsibility of the pastor to make the decisions. He or she primarily will be able to suggest the options available, and to clarify all of the implications of these decisions. The pastor can also ask some questions which no one else might think to ask, or which someone else might feel uncomfortable asking. If the pastor is asked for advice concerning a casket, it is often appropriate to encourage the family to choose a product in a moderate price range. The pastor, however, must be especially sensitive to the needs and feelings of the bereaved and must accept their decisions. This is not a time for the pastor to try and inflict his or her own values or attitudes on the family.

6. The pastor should plan the worship service with the family.

The immediate family should always participate in the planning of the funeral service. This can take place either at the home of the bereaved, or at the office of the pastor, depending on the wishes of the family. At this meeting it is best to discuss all of the issues which surround a funeral service: the music, the Scriptural readings, the eulogy, the sermon, and the burial. More information about specifics can be found in Chapter 14. Also, this meeting with the family is a good opportunity for prayer, which is especially appropriate after reading together some of the great Scriptural passages about resurrection and examining some of the great hymns of the church.

The pastor should point the family toward a funeral service which is centered on the Easter message, on the resurrection of Jesus Christ. There are many hymns which are chosen for funerals which seem to trigger great waves of emotion, but it seems to be far better to choose those hymns which are victorious and triumphant. Other parts of the service also can be laden with emotion, such as the eulogy, or some prayers, or even the sermon. It is important that the pastor encourage those making funeral plans to create a service which is as uplifting and as inspirational as possible. We are not seeking to deny the death, we are not implying that emotional responses are undesirable, but we want to center our worship service on the good news of Jesus Christ.

7. If there is a visitation time at the funeral home, the pastor should be present for at least a part of that event.

Often it is best if the pastor can arrive at the funeral home with the family. To be with the bereaved during the first confrontation with the casket and all it suggests is often very helpful. If there is an open casket for review, the pastor can help the grieving process as the family stands around the casket. Prayer and sharing by the family may also be included at this time.

Sometimes a prayer service or wake is held during the time of visitation. This is usually designed for the family, but often many friends and relatives will be present as well. Here is another opportunity for ministry, and if the family wishes to join in such a service, the pastor should be at the center of the planning process. Again, this is a time for sharing the hope we have in Jesus Christ, a natural time for the reading of Scripture and for prayer. In certain informal settings, this may also be a time when some family members might share memories, insights or faith. The pastor should be as open as possible to any opportunity for ministry, to whatever would be helpful to those who are grieving.

8. The pastor should meet with the family before the funeral or memorial service.

If there is a time for visitation and/or reviewal before the actual service, it is often a good time for the pastor to be present and help comfort those who are grieving. Often this becomes a time of many hugs and embraces, and a time of sharing support and encouragement. The pastor can be especially helpful to those who might be having particular difficulty in dealing with the reality of this death and of the funeral. The pastor might even invite such a person to go for a walk if the pain is too great. Pain is especially prevalent where a casket is present, particularly one which is open.

9. The pastor should strive to see that the funeral or memorial service is carefully planned and conscientiously carried out.

There is no excuse for a sloppy or ill-prepared service. And there are very few events which are as painful as participating in such an experience. A high priority for any pastor is to see that the service is performed with dignity and integrity. The hymns, the Scripture passages, the eulogy, the sermon, the whole event should be designed to lift, inspire and support those who are mourning. The sermon should reflect a sensitivity to the needs of the family, and it should be centered on Christian hope. Even if the person who died was not visibly religious, the pastor's responsibility is to make the service all that it can be. The service is designed for the living. Our message of hope and salvation is universal, applicable in every funeral situation.

We must also be aware that many funeral gatherings contain more people who are unchurched or who do not consider themselves to be Christians than probably any other service at which we might preach during a year. What a marvelous opportunity for us to proclaim the Gospel of Christ, to share the love and hope of the Christian community. There are many examples all around us of how the death of a loved one, or the message at a funeral service, has brought about a dramatic change in the life and faith of a person, sometimes even a new commitment to Christ. Often such an openness at a time like this may not be present at any other point in the lives and attitudes of those who attend.

Thus, we should never underestimate the potential of a funeral service and sermon to impact and change the lives of those in the pews. Our purpose is not exclusively or even primarily evangelical. It is comfort and hope, but if we present the good news of the Gospel, this can certainly be used by God for the change and conversion of people who are present.

10. The pastor should officiate at the burial service.

The service by the graveside is not meant to be a second funeral service, where the pastor has one more crack at saying everything that was left unsaid earlier. This time at the cemetery should be very simple and brief. In cold climates, there is even more reason to keep this time to a minimum.

Scripture and prayer are at the center of the words which are spoken. Often there will be the presentation of the flag, and occasionally some kind of military ceremony will take place. Any other additions to the brief committal service should be strongly discouraged. Following these brief words, it is appropriate for the pastor to greet the family members with a strong handshake or embrace, and to express care and concern for each of them.

Some people today feel strongly that more should be done at the graveside. One school of thought suggests that the casket should be lowered into the grave while the family and friends are present, that this confronts the reality of death more dramatically than walking away while the casket is still above ground. Most funeral directors and cemetery personnel would resist such an emphasis. I personally do not have any strong feelings about the value of such an experience, but certainly would not oppose this if it would be desired by the family.

11. The pastor should continue to be in close contact with the immediate family members of the deceased.

In a sense much of the real work for the pastor begins once the funeral is over, especially as most friends and relatives of the bereaved go back to life as usual. Contact should be made with the grieving family in different ways: visits in the home, calls on the phone, conversations at church, or wherever possible. The pastor should always be alert to the presence of hurting persons, especially those who have lost someone close to them, so that he or she might give personal welcome and support, and might listen to their concerns and expressions of loneliness and pain.

Our congregation has a time for prayer each Sunday morning, usually just before the close of the worship service. At this time we invite anyone who would like to come to the altar rail and kneel with the pastors during this time of prayer. The pastor leads the congregation in prayer, but participants in worship also have an opportunity to come forward and kneel. We often encourage families who are in grief to be among those who kneel, and we remember them by name in the prayers for comfort and healing. It is good for the congregation to actually see those who are going through grief, so that personal support and love may be shared as a part of the Sunday morning worship.

Pastors should have two primary goals in their contact with the bereaved. These are crucially important. First, we need to avoid at all costs falling back on pious platitudes. For instance, some pastors have been known to say, "Your loved one is much better off now," or, "You will get over this soon," or, "You will be a much stronger person because of this experience." Some have even implied that this death was somehow God's will. The wise pastor does far more listening than talking, hearing the personal story of pain and heartache, or the feelings of anger and abandonment which are often present. The pastor can also give or lend books to the bereaved which might be helpful, such as *When a Loved One Dies* by Phillip Williams, *You and Your Grief* by Edgar Jackson, or *Good Grief* by Granger Westberg.

The second goal pastors should have is to continue to mention the deceased by name. So many people will avoid talking about the person who has died because it is believed that this will generate all sorts of sad feelings among the survivors. In talking about the person who has died, however, the bereaved are able to work through their grief. In telling the story again and again people are healed. This is not a quick process; some counselors suggest that it takes a minimum of six to ten hours of discussing the loss with a caring, non-judgmental person, most likely over an extended period of time, for someone in grief to begin to work it all through. This area is one of the pastor's most important ministries.

12. The pastor should help to create a wider support base where it is needed.

The pastor cannot and should not try to do all of the grief work in a congregation. Thus, it is important to train and equip others to be there at the times of death and sorrow. One of the best programs we have discovered for this purpose is that of the Stephen Ministry, a healing approach which comes to us from St. Louis, Missouri. We first learned of this from a Roman Catholic parish nearby, but now many congregations in our community are involved.

There are other examples of training people to be caregivers, of equipping and enabling them to do much of the congregation's ministry, but the Stephen Ministry is a wonderful way for pastors to reproduce the ministry. After persons are given the necessary skills, they are then assigned to individuals who might need the love and support of this ministry for a period of time. A grieving person needs these caregivers.

A congregation should also consider establishing a grief support group. Many such gatherings meet in both congregations and hospitals, and these can be invaluable to the bereaved. Howard Clinebell, a well-known author and counselor, suggests that such grief support groups be no more than ten persons and be led by someone who has some group skills. Each person in the group should be encouraged to share his or her deepest hurt, followed by an opportunity for the others in the group to express a reaction to this hurt in words or action. This process continues until each person has shared, and all of the other members have responded. In this way, he says, there can be a real healing which takes place; no one goes home without having been truly heard.

Clearly, if a grieving person is not able to work through the pain and loss, not able to deal with the reality of this new situation, then it is sometimes necessary to recommend professional help. There are some very fine counselors in most larger communities, sometimes at hospitals, at counseling centers or even at other churches. We should not be hesitant to recommend such resources; we cannot do everything ourselves.

But for the most part, a congregation and a pastor have all the resources that are needed to support a person who is experiencing the death of a loved one. In fact, we are very often much better at this than we might imagine; we have learned a great deal in the church about how to respond and how to be truly helpful. Jesus provides the external example of compassion, of love, showing the direction each congregation should travel. It usually remains, however, for the pastor to place a high priority on this aspect of ministry, and to share this understanding and insight with the whole congregation.

GRIEVING AFTER A DEATH

*W*hen a death breaks into the life of a family, those who have been closest to the deceased are in a period of grief. This is a natural and normal situation, and we should not be at all surprised. When we are separated from a loved one by death, we mourn. It hurts. The death of one who has been close to us is among the most painful events that we can ever experience. Grief by its very nature is painful and difficult. As Christians, we may be different because of the hope of the resurrection that we possess, but this does not take away the hurt. At the time of death, a universal reaction is the presence of grief.

In the past two decades, the person who has had the greatest influence on our understanding of grief has been Dr. Elizabeth Kubler-Ross. In her bestselling book, *Death and Dying*, she outlined what she called the stages of grief. These included the familiar experiences of denial, anger, bargaining, depression, and then finally acceptance. We have heard these stages described so often that many have almost assumed that these are eternal principles, almost sacred. And there is a close link with reality in what she describes and suggests.

However, in recent years there has been increasing debate about and challenge to these conclusions. While at the same time appreciating the pioneer efforts of Dr. Kubler-Ross, especially in bringing the whole arena of death and grief to public consciousness, there are many who think that she has missed the boat in some areas. What is particularly under challenge today is her conviction that dying and grief are essentially a time of growth. Under question is her assumption that people move through some rather predictable stages until there is the final stage of growth as death comes near. In other words, people are taking issue on her contention that death and dying and grief are inherently a time of development, of moving forward, of discovering a new and more rewarding maturity and understanding.

There is the growing belief, however, that this is not what happens during the dying or grief process. When a person is dying, to say that imminent death rather automatically or mechanically brings about some kind of psychological or emotional growth is not borne out by experience. Often physical pain and deterioration of the body cause psychological distress and regression, not some ideal of growth. People may indeed grow during the dying process, and often do, but this is not necessarily the case, nor is it clear this should always be the goal. Is peaceful acceptance of dying that ideal toward which we strive, or should there be something else inside of the person which continues to struggle to live?

From a Christian perspective, it is also highly questionable whether death is the final stage of growth. In the Bible death is often seen as a terrible and painful disruption of the gift of life. Jesus gives ample evidence of the pain and agony of dying when he cries out in the words of Psalm 22, *"My God, my God, why have you forsaken me?"* These are hardly the words of stoic resignation and passive acceptance.

In addition, Dr. Kubler-Ross suggests that the final stage of growth, the stage of acceptance, is a time of detachment and separation from those who have been closest in life. It suggests a virtual cutting off of all ties with this world, and with the relationships which have been so important. There is the stated goal of some form of emotional self-sufficiency. However, in effect, she is legitimating the emotional and even physical abandonment of the dying. She goes on to suggest that the terror and pain of death and dying can be diminished if we only understand the various stages that accompany this event. In other words, if we only understand the death process, then we will be able to accept death. Coupled with this assertion, she criticizes religion as being a defense against the true acceptance of death.

In contradiction to Dr. Kubler-Ross' conclusions, I would strongly suggest that death and dying are more a process than a movement through various stages. We do not walk along some continuum, progressing through stages. I believe that the process of dying is instead made up of a series of emotional, psychological and perhaps physical crises and experiences, which come and go all the way through this period in our lives. Just about the time we believe we may have reached some form of acceptance, then something sends us almost all the way back to the beginning of the process.

In addition, I am not at all sure that acceptance of dying is to be our goal, that the end result is to be able to find some kind of serenity and peace. That may happen for many, but for others death may not be at all peaceful; it may involve a tremendous struggle and turmoil, for we desperately want to live. Death in the Scriptures is often portrayed more as an enemy than as a friend. While we have hope for eternal life, that does not make dying any less traumatic. We are not like the soldiers of Iran who walk gladly into battle so they might give up their lives for a better place beyond. We find life to be very precious, and we struggle to live.

Also, in terms of the dying process, from a Christian perspective there is little truth in the assertion that the goal of dying is to achieve some form of emotional isolation. Rather, it is abundantly clear that the most important dynamic for the dying person is the presence and support of loving people. The dying do not need less people contact; they need *more*. A loving person, sitting by the bedside of one who is dying, holding the hand, stroking the brow, sharing hope and love and faith, is much more the picture of the Christian understanding of death than any image of growth from emotional isolation.

It is true that much of the writings of Dr. Kubler-Ross deal with the situation of one who is dying, while the purpose of this book is to primarily focus on the reality which is present after a death has taken place. But there are some strong similarities in the grieving which goes on in a death, during a period in which someone close to us is dying, and the grief which follows the death. Grief is grief, and has some similar dynamics whenever it takes place. However, it is now time to look more closely at the grief process which reaches its fullest dimension after a death has taken place.

What is grief? Grief is an emotion. It involves the feeling life of a person. It is felt deep inside as a tearing kind of experience; there is something ripped out of us that cannot be put back. As we feel this sensation deep inside of us, it is almost impossible to explain or define it to anyone else. Grief is also psychic pain; the center of our being really hurts.

Some analogies have been used to describe the nature of grief. It has been treated at times as being like a medical problem, an illness, even a disease. A person in grief is sick, and what is needed is to get well. We sometimes ask people in grief if they are feeling better, is the illness almost gone. Perhaps a vacation or a few days off will bring about healing from this temporary condition of pain. Maybe even a medication might be the answer.

Another analogy is found in the world of sports. When a person is injured in an athletic contest, we often call this "going down with an injury". The team doctors rush in and drag the person off the field and into the dressing room. The goal of that medical person is to get the player back into the game as soon as possible, the same day or at least by the next game. So we view the grieving person as injured for a day or two, and we want to get him or her back into the game of life as soon as possible. By rushing people back too soon we run the risk of making an injury even worse; but we believe that if someone is really tough, especially determined, that person will not lose much playing time.

However, grief is more than an illness or an injury. Much more. Perhaps a better analogy would be that of an amputation. If any of us would have to lose a limb, an arm or a leg, we might ask ourselves how long it would be before we were ready to be "whole" again. How long would it take for us truly to adjust to this radically different situation? Can this situation be solved by a few bandaids and a book on positive thinking? The answer is no. Grief is a process that involves incredible pain, heartache and disruption. It does not go away in a few days or even a few weeks.

What dynamics are usually present at the time of grief?

1. Shock

The first emotional response to the death of a loved one is what we call shock. Shock means that some of our pain is shut off, as if we had been given an anesthetic. There is a sense of unreality, as if we were living in a dream, or more accurately, a nightmare. We may be numb all over. Panic and sheer fright may set in. Our emotions can be out of control, irrational and unpredictable.

We cannot rehearse for the sudden and surprising grief which pours upon us. We can only truly learn about it after it arrives. Shock is almost like coming very close to a hot object such as a stove, or a live electrical wire, instinctively drawing back from the potential hurt. Shock is drawing back from the reality of death. The brain says to the body that this is just too much for it to stand, it is time to leave. Emotional leave-taking is called shock.

Shock can be a good gift from God. Lasting anywhere from a couple of days to two weeks or more, shock protects us from receiving the full impact all at once. We are unable to comprehend totally the meaning of the loss of a person close to us, and shock helps us walk through those first hours and days. We need that kind of shock very much, but only for a while.

During this initial time of grief, many physical side effects often accompany shock. We may be absolutely speechless, as if struck by a thunderbolt. This is accentuated in situations where a person did not witness the death, or did not anticipate its coming. There is a wide difference between watching someone die on a sickbed, and being awakened one evening with the news about a fatal accident.

There is often the physical impulse to throw oneself into a heap—some people faint dead away. Shock brings about disorientation; people have a hard time thinking clearly or performing even menial tasks. There may be pain in the stomach, cramps and indigestion. There can be such symptoms as dizziness, blurred vision, palpitations, chest pains or shortness of breath. We may truly hurt all over.

What we need to remember about the time of shock is that this is perfectly normal. Shock is a protective part of the human condition. All of life is suddenly thrown out of balance. The closer we were to the person who died, the more havoc this period of time will create. It is important to realize that the feelings of shock will not last, and that there are many individual differences as to shock's effect on persons. Death is almost always a shock.

2. Emotional Turmoil and Upheaval

After the initial shock, there is a period of time in which a person faces some erratic or even frightening emotions. A person never seems to know what emotional outburst will come next. These emotions often arrive in waves. This time of emotional uncertainty can last for some time, usually taking place as soon as the shock has worn off and lasting until the fourth or fifth month after the death. It is a time when much support, love and encouragement are needed, when there is someone close by who will truly listen and empathize. It is a very emotional period in a person's life, probably with an intensity of feelings that goes beyond anything previously experienced.

Some of the emotional responses which are most common include:

Tears

As the emotional overload sweeps over us, the tears usually flow freely. The dam bursts, and everything just comes pouring out. This is a very healthy response to grief. God gave us tear ducts to help us express our emotions, so that we can find healing and release through tears. A person who is able to weep in the midst of this period of emotional upheaval is usually a person who is going through "good grief".

Unfortunately, in our culture there is a tendency to try and suppress any outbursts of tears. We have been given very clearly the message that tears make many people uncomfortable. They are embarrassing or frightening to some. Little children are more free to cry than adults, and women are more able to cry than most men. Christians often see tears as a demonstration of a lack of faith.

However, one of the most graphic biblical illustrations of grief and tears is in John 11:35 when Jesus wept. His friend Lazarus had died, Mary and Martha were emotionally overloaded, and Jesus released his pain through tears. We always have the choice of suppressing, repressing or expressing, and the latter is always the best. Grief makes us want to cry.

Denial
One of the most common emotions and attitudes that is present at the time of death is that of refusing to believe that it has happened. "It cannot be" and "I can't believe it" are common language. We have a tendency to deny anything which is too painful or upsetting in our lives, and death obviously would be at the top of the list. We believe that if we will not accept the fact, then maybe it will not really be true.

Amazingly, we use denial language through much of the death experience. People talk about the loved one as having passed away, or passed on. Some even say that the person expired, whatever that means. I personally would rather die than expire. We sometimes praise those who go through a funeral service without expressing much emotion. We hold up a Jackie Kennedy as the ideal who kept her composure at the funeral of her husband. We see these individuals as strong, courageous and filled with faith. Perhaps there is some truth in this, but it also could mean that denial is very much present. We need not be cool heroes when death comes.

Professor Walt Bouman of Trinity Seminary in Columbus, Ohio, talks about four evidences of denial which are present in our culture.

1. Americans by and large do not talk about death. Even people who are dying do not talk about it. It is parallel to some elements of the life insurance industry, which goes along with not talking about death. Obviously it is death insurance that they are selling, but death is not mentioned. A favorite statement of many in the industry is this, "If something should happen to you . . ." "If something should happen to

you." What do we think is going to happen to us? We know we will die, but we deny that reality.

2. Our culture focuses primarily on youth and ignores those who are aged. Our media glamorize youth; the advertizing industry idealizes it. At times we almost believe that unless we are youthful we are missing the essence of life. But as we continue to age, to grow older, to move beyond our youth, we wonder why there is such a conspiracy of silence. It is part of our denial.

3. We have tended to hide death in hospitals, in nursing homes, away from the mainstream of life. Two generations ago almost all of us would have experienced death in our own home, or at least in the immediate family. We probably would have seen someone die. But death has been banished to those places where people are out of sight, and therefore out of mind. It is a form of denial.

4. The whole funeral industry engages in a ritual of denial. Our burial procedures do not emphasize the reality of the death, but rather the preservation of the body. There is a waterproof and rubber sealed casket, special locks for proection, as well as a seepage-proof vault. But what is all this protection *for*? It is the denial of death.

Then there are all the images present in the industry. We concentrate on rest and comfort, sleep and preservation. Caskets have inner spring mattresses with foam rubber pillows. Euphemisms abound, as we encounter slumber rooms, memorial gardens, rest havens. The industry, according to Professor Bouman, would like us to believe that it is confronting death, helping people to work through this reality, but it seems instead often a denial that the event has actually happened.

Guilt

An emotion which appears to be present at almost every funeral is that of guilt. We seem to have an abundance of guilt in the center of our beings in the first place, and there is nothing like a death to further bring it out. Sometimes I am afraid that these feelings of guilt lead to the purchase of very expensive funerals, as loved ones wish to deal with that sense of guilt by some last act of love or respect.

Guilt is so often present because there is hardly a person who cannot remember things that were said to the person who died which probably should not have been said, or things not said that should have been communicated. We can always find some "Why didn't I" comments to confront, and guilt can be the result. There is also guilt among many who feel that somehow another action might have saved the life of the deceased. "If only" the survivor would have noticed this, or done that, or said something else, this person would still be alive today. Guilt is often prominent.

Anger

Death often brings a feeling of utter helplessness, of powerlessness, which in turn often evokes feelings of anger. We do not like to be helpless, or abandoned, so we lash out. This anger can be felt either like an erupting volcano or a slow burn. There can be a general irritability or a lingering bitterness. We often feel that someone has to be responsible for this death: the doctor, the pastor, even God. We also can become angry at the person who died. That sounds rather bizarre, but it is exactly what happens. "How could you leave me alone?" is the feeling that is present.

Anger should be expressed, finding release from the pain by getting it out. Dr. Alvin Rogness writes, after the death of his son, that he found some comfort in anger. In his anger at what had happened to the world, he could understand something of God's frustration and pain at also watching his Son die, at watching things go awry in the world. Dr. Rogness found comfort in knowing that God was also grieving, that he was in sorrow and had tears in his eyes. Anger is normal at the time of death.

3. Acceptance and Resistance

This is a time of both going forward and retreating, of moving on and moving backward. It is a time when pain can be intense, and when the hurt can almost be gone. This period of grief most often occurs from the fourth or fifth month after the death to well beyond a year, sometimes lasting as long as 18 months. This extended period of time is most often a time of healing. Often the fifth to the ninth month are the most difficult to experience. The gaping wound that has been inflicted by the death is now felt in all of its intensity.

Meanwhile, most of the people who were so supportive and encouraging during the first months of grief have now gone back to life as usual. They are less empathetic and understanding. Often they become impatient with the lack of "progress" they see. Most do not understand the grief process and feel that by this time it should be mostly over. If the bereaved person is having a hard time, some of these friends or family might even give some free lectures to them: "It is time to snap out of this, to move on." Usually, however, such a response by those who were so supportive just makes this more difficult.

Dr. Rogness, in his book *Appointment with Death*, shares some of his theological insights which gave him hope and comfort during this struggle with acceptance. I paraphrase from several pages of the book:

They are gone, but they are not gone. They are with God in glory. They have disappeared over the hill, they have rounded the bend, we see them no longer. But they are not annihilated. They have been put on their feet again, to serve God and to enjoy him forever in the more glorious sectors of his kingdom. Are they now beyond our reach and are we beyond theirs? And who are we to say that the veil that separates the living from the dead may not be a very thin one. Shall we limit God?

In the 11th chapter of Hebrews, the writer parades a long list of people who have lived and died in the Lord. Then in the opening of the 12th chapter, the author presents us with this rapturous picture of the "bleachers". Seeing we are surrounded by so great a cloud of witnesses, let us lay aside every weight and the sin which easily besets us, and let us run with patience the race that is set before us.

We are the runners who are still out on the track. They have run the race and won and now become the cheering section for us. We leave ourselves much the poorer if we neglect the support, the pressure, and the encouragement of the bleachers.

The bleachers came to my help. I pictured my son among the great sea of indistinguishable faces, cheering me on. "On with the race, Dad. Now you are making it." To surrender the bleachers is to leave one with memories only, or with just items to cherish. A major part of history has in its liturgies kept open the lanes of traffic between the saints on this side, and the saints on the other. The magnificent bleacher lines in Hebrews continue to look to Jesus, the author and finisher of our faith, the inspiration, the strength, the comforter and the hope we need for our peace, that is set before us.

In conclusion he writes, They are gone, but they are not gone. They now belong to the bleachers. Is there hope? I confess that I believe in the resurrection of the dead and the life of the world to come. Each of us in his time will have to get along without this world. The final turn in the road is not the final one at all. Beyond death, vistas only broaden. The goodness and beauty of life, tasted here, will be given in all their fullness there.

4. Assimilation and Integration

This is the point at which grieving persons now regain a good deal of energy, optimism and hope that had been crushed in the pain of the death. They now see themselves as moving closer to recovery, and the self image changes. They are more drawn to their own future, and begin to reinvest themselves in life. This usually takes place between the first year or year-and-a-half after the death, and up to three years. Now it becomes easier to look to the future than to the past.

The survivors do not forget the person who has died, but now move the grieving from the foreground to the background. They have less need to talk about the deceased, are less preoccupied with the belongings, and do not need to dwell as much on memories or stories of the person who has died. The loss is not any less real, but the sense of impoverishment is abating. The person begins to feel whole again, and the sense of normality is returning.

Sometimes this takes longer than three years. Judy Tatel-baum, in her excellent book *The Courage to Grieve*, shares how she held on to her grief for her dead brother for some 14 years. Then she goes on to share in rather moving fashion how she finally was able to let this pain go. The scene she describes is a group counseling session, and I paraphrase from parts of this:

I was angry at my brother for dying. When I shared this the leader put an empty chair in front of me and said, "Tell your brother that you are angry at him for dying." I gasped. What a confrontation! I wanted to run away and hide. Although I had cried and cried over David's death, never before had I acknowl-edged in any way that I might have been angry at poor David for dying. I felt very shaken.

I began very unsure, "David, I am angry at you for dying." Suddenly a flood of feelings emerged. Mainly I felt angry that David had died before teaching me the things about boys and dating that as an older brother he had promised to teach me. I felt angry that he left me when I was feeling so vulner-able, that he had left me feeling so responsible for being the only child now with my parents, that he had left me lonely, and that he was gone and would never come back to be with me again.

Up to that moment, anger at David seemed wrong, inap-propriate, selfish, and unfair. Now I cried with pain and relief. My sorrow had been well expressed many times before; it was my anger which seemed totally new.

The leader paused and said, "Now say good-bye to David." I know I must have looked at him with horror. Good-bye seemed like a terrible word. However, in that moment I saw how I had clung to my dead brother for years, how I had been preoccupied with him, how I had pretended that he was with me and held on to him for dear life instead of fully living alone without him. It was a frightening moment.

I asked the leader what would happen to me if I said good-bye to David, imagining that a crash of thunder or some other frightening phenomenon would occur. He calmly said that he did not know what would happen, that I would have to risk finding out for myself by saying good-bye.

I hesitated further and the leader said, "Perhaps you aren't ready." I heard this as a challenge. I imagined that he thought I was too immature or gutless to say good-bye. I said, "I want to be ready now," and then I turned to the empty chair that represented my brother and said, "Good-bye, David."

To my amazement, nothing special happened at all, neither the anticipated thunder nor any special feeling inside of me. I told the leader that I felt empty, that I was surprised to not have more emotion in my dreaded good-bye. The leader said, "Try this. Say 'Good-bye, David' and then 'Hello, world.'"

I silently reflected that his suggestion sounded crazy. However, since I had agreed to take the further risk, I did as he suggested and said, "Good-bye, David. Hello, world." I looked up at the group of people sitting in the circle around me, who had not existed for me until that moment. I saw tears streaming down many of their faces as I said, "Hello, world."

I jumped up and ran over to look at them more closely, to touch their tears. I was deeply moved to have so many people crying for me and with me. Then I experienced a joy I had never known before. I felt alive in a beautiful world of loving people. Alive was wonderful.

The moment was a turning point in my life. After 14 years of grieving, I had faced painful, formerly unacceptable feelings, said good-bye to my brother and fully rejoined the living. My chronic depression dissipated. My life has become better and better ever since.

In summary, there are two basic goals in the whole grieving process. The first is to acknowledge the truth of what has happened, that a death has occurred, and that the relationship is now over. The second test is to experience and deal with all of the emotions and feelings and problems which this death creates for the bereaved. It does not happen overnight; it may take three years or more before one is truly ready to leave grief behind. But there will come a time when a person can start over again, when the sun will shine, when life will be beautiful. This is the hope that should be with us as we grieve.

SUICIDE

*I*t is not the intention of this book to spend much time on the various causes of death in our society. Much could be written about the way people die, about the issues of medical ethics and euthanasia and other related subjects. One could also deal with accidental death and examine the dangers of the world in which we live. But in order to give this any kind of credible and effective treatment, it would take far more time and space than we have here, so it must remain for someone else to research.

However, there is one cause of death that should not be ignored. This is the tragic reality of suicide. This is a crisis which has long been ignored, not only by society as a whole, but also by much of the Christian community. For instance, some recent books I have read on death do not even mention suicide. Many Bible dictionaries and commentaries give virtually no insight or help. We basically have chosen to simply ignore the fact that many people are indeed taking their own lives.

However, for those of us who minister day in and day out to people in pain, we know that suicide is an ever-growing reality in our midst. Hardly a week goes by that we do not hear about some suicide attempt in the vicinity where we live and work. At times it even comes right into the middle of our congregations, and we are faced with the immediacy of such a tragedy.

Most parish pastors have been put into the difficult situation of dealing with a suicide in the congregation or in the surrounding community. This usually means that a funeral must be planned, a family must be given ministry, and a funeral sermon must be preached. What do we say or do? What is an appropriate word from the Lord at the time of a suicide? As most of us know, there is very little help available in any kind of Christian literature at the present time.

The church throughout history has struggled with the tragedy of suicide, and often the response has been less than helpful. The venerable John Wesley wrote in the late 18th century, as suicide reached epidemic proportions:

"There is no country in Europe, or perhaps in the in- habitable world, where the horrid crime of self-murder is so common as it is in England! . . . But how can this vile abuse of the law be prevented, and this execrable crime effectually discouraged?

Let a law be made and rigorously executed, that the body of every self-murderer, Lord or peasant, shall be hanged in chains, and the English fury will cease at once."

I would suggest that appealing to such leaders from the past is not very productive or helpful. Wesley's grand solution was not only ineffective in stopping suicide, but was designed to create inestimable pain and suffering for the surviving families. I find his lack of sensitivity and compassion to be appalling, but realize that the contemporary church has often paralleled this harsh and vin- dictive spirit. Christ's love and mercy have been tragically over- looked by so many who claim to be speaking for the Gospel and for Jesus Christ. I think today is the right time to look at suicide in a new way in the church.

By way of introduction, it is important that we realize how wide- spread this phenomenon has become. Suicide is certainly evidence of the amount of pain and suffering that is present in our midst. Suicide affects all age groups. For instance, some 25% of all suicides are committed by persons who are over the age of 65. The highest rate of suicide is among white males who are in their 80s.

Suicide, however, is increasing most dramatically among the young. At the present time it is the second most common cause of death among teenagers, ranking just behind that of automobile accidents. And it is estimated that many of the car accidents are also, in effect, suicides. The overall estimate today in America is that there are between 400,000 and 500,000 attempted suicides by young people each year, and at least 10% of these succeed. Females are five times more likely to attempt suicide than males, but of the males who make the attempt, they are five times more likely to succeed than females.

Why do suicides take place, and why are they becoming more frequent? Between 1950 and 1980 the rate of suicide tripled. Perhaps it is because our world has become a more complex and painful place to live. But specifically, why do suicides take place, and what causes people to take this drastic action? Causes that seem to be most prevalent include the following:

1. One major cause of suicide seems to be the overriding influence of television. Studies show that the amount of violence and conflict on TV does have an impact on those who watch. With the average person watching seven hours or more of television a day, eventually this can change and warp the values of a society. When you see death and destruction and hopelessness so often on the tube, it becomes easier to see the dark side in oneself, to lose the capacity to hope and believe in the value of life.

2. Suicide is caused by the presence of some form of grief, grief over some loss. Often a suicide attempt will take place soon after some relationship has ended, after some form of rejection or abandonment. It appears to the person in the midst of this pain that life is no longer worth living, it is time to get out.

3. Suicide is caused by a desire for revenge, an action designed to get even with those who have created conflict or pain in that person's life. It may be a parent or child who has been the source of irritation or misery, and this gives a person a chance to truly get even. It has a double purpose; it is an opportunity to get away from the hassles and hurt and, at the same time, inflict maximum pain on those who have been perceived as being in some way responsible for this situation.

4. Suicide is caused by abuse which has happened in a person's life. We are now becoming much more aware of all of the physical, mental and sexual abuse that is present in our society. Often the scars and pain from this abuse as a child or an adult are just too painful to live with any longer, so the person decides to leave.

5. Suicide is caused by developmental changes in life, those times of transition when everything seems to be in upheaval. The teenager is being shoved out of the security of the family and is now having to fly solo, or the older person is now facing retirement and dealing with a sense of self worth. It is often a time of moving from the familiar to the unfamiliar.

6. Suicide is caused by the influence of chemicals. The rate of those attempting suicide among this group is estimated to be at least 30% higher than the national average. With the increased consumption of alcohol nationwide, with the almost epidemic proportions of chemical abuse in many different forms, suicide rates will continue to rise until we have dealt forcefully with chemical abuse.

7. Suicide is caused by various kinds of mental or emotional depression. It is probably true that people who commit suicide display symptoms of depression more than any other single characteristic. Child psychologists now speak of "early onset depression" in children, some who manifest suicidal tendencies as young as age three. Many of these children will attempt suicide several times before the age of ten. Depression, however, affects those of all ages, and will often lead a person to contemplate or even attempt suicide.

8. Suicide is more prevalent in those families where suicide has occurred in the past. It seems as if a person who has experienced suicide in the family should be strongly committed to seeing that it should not happen again. However, it is a fact that children who come from a family where suicide has happened are more likely to attempt it on their own.

9. Suicide happens far more often among people who have already made previous attempts. It is easier, not harder to try a second time and a third time. The most vulnerable time seems to be during the first two years after a previous attempt.

10. Suicide is more common in those who have made suicidal threats. Sometimes we do not take these seriously, and this is a mistake. All suicidal talk and prediction by a person should be taken with seriousness. Most people who commit suicide have talked about it with someone in the past, although there are certainly exceptions to this.

11. Suicide is common among those who begin to make final arrangements for their life, who begin to give away treasured possessions and become preoccupied with the event of leaving this earth.

12. Suicide often occurs among people who have gone through some very definitive behavioral change. We can see some rather pronounced changes in dress, in behavior, in attitude, in personality, in relationships. This is usually a sign that inner turmoil is at work and often leads to the kind of despair and anxiety which can become self-destructive.

13. Suicide is often accompanied by some kind of self-defeating behavior. The person may not be able to keep a job, may alienate many people that have been close, may begin to drink obsessively, and even may drive recklessly. There seems to be something within that is seeking to find destruction, and suicide can be a logical extension of this behavior.

14. Suicide is sometimes caused by some kind of physical problem in a person's life — a disability, a serious illness, an unwanted pregnancy, the threat of serious surgery, or the fear of any of the above. Sometimes those who cannot cope with the threats to their physical well-being find it easier to run away, for good.

There are certainly other reasons why people take their own life. Also, many of the above occur together. It is good, however, for all of us to know something of what might cause this kind of attempt, and to try and alleviate some of these tensions as they arise. The Christian community can be extremely helpful in bringing about an awareness of the hope we have in Jesus Christ, the hope that we have been given, the value and worth of human life. We can do much preventative work before suicide rears its ugly head. This can begin right now.

I have always been intrigued to read about the last days of Jesus' life before the crucifixion, seeing these in terms of suicide. The disciple Peter was a blustery, proud, and impulsive man. When Jesus talked to him about loyalty and devotion, Peter was the one who promised he would never desert, never deny. But then, at the time of the arrest of Jesus, Peter is found denying his Lord three times in the space of one evening. These were not just casual denials, sins of omission or a loss of memory. These were intense, bitter denials of any association with the one called Jesus, and by the time the cock crowed three times, Peter was in shambles. He was shamed and ashamed. Suicide would not have been out of the question for someone who had fallen so far, who was hurting so badly.

Yet the overwhelming reality of that event was that Peter was not abandoned by the others. He was taken into the center of that group of followers, even though he denied his Lord from the very center of his being. And in this healing group, Peter experienced the magnificent grace and forgiveness of God. Later on in John 21 Jesus will lead Peter very carefully and gracefully through a time of three-fold affirmation, paralleling the three-fold denial. The words of Jesus, *"Peter, feed my sheep,"* will never leave Peter for the rest of his life. At the time of his greatest pain, Peter was surrounded and loved.

On the other hand, there was Judas. He too was a betrayer, who sold our his Lord for just a few pieces of silver. A tragic picture is painted. After the crucifixion, Judas is devastated. He throws away the coins which had been given him, finding that any hope or meaning has vanished. We see no evidence that anyone reached out to him in his pain. No one went to him, embraced him and assured him of the power of forgiveness. Judas was abandoned, and in his isolation he went out and took his own life.

We as the Christian community cannot let people go. We cannot sit back and watch those people who show self-destructive tendencies go and act on them. We must reach out in love and compassion. In those circumstances where all ministry seems to bear no fruit, however, where a suicide results, then we cannot let go of the grieving family. We cannot abandon people at this point of need.

Let me suggest four guidelines for congregations and pastors at the time of a suicide:

1. Respond in compassion and love.

The pain that is suffered by the grieving family is beyond anything we could ever comprehend. The guilt, despair and depression that is present is beyond measure. Thus, if ever there was a time when we should be compassionate and understanding, this is it. The pastor should be willing to do all that is listed in the chapter on the role of the pastor, and more. This is more than a "usual" death; there is shame, helplessness, bitterness and anguish which transcend any other death. We cannot help but respond as disciples of Christ.

2. Plan and implement a Christian funeral in the church.

Any congregation which refuses to host a funeral service for one who has committed a suicide is simply causing more pain to those who are already deeply hurt. I find nothing in the Scriptures which condones such behavior on the part of the Christian community. We have just out-Phariseed the Pharisees, and attempted to be like God in our judgment. It seems to me that was the sin of Adam and Eve. This should be the time when we present the unconditional love of Jesus Christ in all of its fullness and power.

3. Refuse any temptation to make judgments about the person who has died.

Any comments that might be made about condemnation or questioning the salvation of the person are completely inappropriate. In my own experience, in almost every suicide situation, those who have died have been filled with incredible internal pain, far beyond what any of us who survived could imagine. Something snapped inside. These individuals were out of control. It is not up to us to make any judgments, but to assure the survivors of God's love and mercy. Read Romans 8, *"For I am convinced that nothing in all the world, neither death nor life, nor angels nor principalities, nor things present nor things to come, nor height nor depth nor anything else in all creation will be able to separate us from the love of God in Christ Jesus."* That is the promise we have, and that is all we can or should say at such a time.

4. Do everything possible in the Christian community to help the grieving family move through the time of grief.

No one should be abandoned at the time of death, but in the case of suicide survivors are often tempted to isolate themselves, to cut themselves off from other human beings, to suffer guilt, shame and pain alone. We need to be in touch, to surround them with all of the resources that are a part of our faith and life, and make sure that we hold our arms very tightly around them. Those who are alone at the time of a suicide are really alone. We are given the task of helping in that loneliness.

In closing, I would like to repeat the words that I preached at the funeral of a person who committed suicide, a young woman who had been in the midst of much personal turmoil and pain. I hope this will be an example of an approach and a message for this kind of event in a parish.

As we join together this afternoon as this most difficult hour, we have in common many deep and painful feelings. We experience today, for instance, the feeling of grief, because one who has been special to us is no longer here. We grieve because death brings separation, and there is nothing more painful in this life than separation.

We also experience the feelings of guilt. We all wonder and worry in our own minds whether there was not something more that we could have done. We feel guilty because of things we did or did not do, or because of words that we did or did not say. We are asking questions of ourselves today, asking whether we did everything we could have done for Mary. And I know as one who was close to her, we cannot dismiss these questions as easily as we would like. "Could we have done something different?" or "Could we have done more?" We feel the guilt of this hour.

We also feel failure. We feel failure because it is obvious that in recent months and weeks none has truly understood the depth of turmoil and pain in Mary's life. We feel failure because we were unable to show her all of the reasons she had to live, and how much we needed her.

And we feel loneliness. There is an emptiness about today, a void that really nothing can fill. We wish so much that we could turn the clock back a week, a year, a decade, but that is not possible. We are very lonely.

And we also feel wounded and hurt.

In addition to feelings, we also have many questions today. I would center on just two of them. The first question that most of us is asking is simply, "Why?" Why did death have to come so early in her life? Why could she not have spent many, many more years in our family? Why? I don't have a complete answer; we leave that to God. But I do believe that Mary was suffering from an illness, that deep down inside of her she was experiencing a disabling disease that none of us could ever understand.

Her illness was as real as cancer or heart disease, and it made her a stranger to all of us, to the world, and even to herself. If we ask the question, "What caused Mary to become sick?" we have no answer. But if we ask, "Why did her life end so prematurely?" we can say, "It was because she had a serious and even fatal illness."

This may not change our feelings of guilt and failure, at least not right away. But here is where we need to turn our attention away from our own feelings to the Gospel of Jesus Christ. Here is where we need to hear loudly and clearly that we worship, we love and serve a God who is merciful, forgiving, loving and the source of all new life. We cling more than ever to the words of Jesus when he said, *"Come unto me all who labor and are burdened, and I will give you rest" (Matthew 11:28).*

Into our feelings of remorse and sadness come one word of Scripture after another:

Psalm 23
"Even though I walk through the valley of the shadow of death, I will fear no evil, for thou art with me."

Psalm 103
"He does not deal with us according to our sins, for as the heavens are high above the earth, so great is his steadfast love

toward those who fear him, as far as the east is from the west, so far does he remove our transgressions from us."

Isaiah 43

"Fear not, for I have redeemed you, I have called you by name, and you are mine. When you pass through the waters I will be with you; and through the rivers, they shall not overwhelm you, when you walk through fire you shall not be burned."

John 14

"Peace I leave with you, my peace I give to you, not as the world gives do I give to you. Let not your hearts be troubled, neither let them be afraid."

1 John 3

"If our conscience condemns us, we know that God is greater than our conscience and that he knows everything."

John 16

"So you have sorrow now, but I will see you again and your hearts will rejoice, and no one will ever take your joy from you."

2 Corinthians 1

"Blessed be the God and Father of our Lord Jesus Christ, the Father of Mercies, and God of all comfort who comforts us in all of our affliction. For as we share abundantly in Christ's sufferings, so through Christ we share abundantly in comfort too."

To Mary's family, the words of Romans 15 are in each of us today as we rejoice with those who rejoice and we weep with those who weep. You are surrounded and held and loved by those in the Christian community who are here and by many all over the world. Above all, you are not alone.

You may be terribly lonely, but you are not alone. For Christ has chosen to live in the lives of people, and we wish to share with you the reality of that presence. Let each of us bear at least a small part of your heavy burden.

The second question is this, "What is the meaning of death, Mary's death?" It would be much easier to find the meaning of her life, her joy, her love for others, her compassion for her family and friends, her faith in Christ, her relationships with each of us. But what about the meaning of her death?

At this point we have nowhere to turn except to the promises of God. In a sense this is true of life also; there is no meaning outside of the promises of God. But at the time of death, our focus is completely on this awareness. The only way to understand the meaning of death is to lift our eyes from the casket and gaze upon the cross.

Let me read those victorious words from Romans 8, *"Who, then can separate us from the love of Christ? Can trouble do it, or hardship, or persecution, or hunger or poverty or danger or death. No, in all these things we have complete victory through him who loved us.*

For I am certain that nothing can separate us from his love, neither life nor death, neither angels nor other heavenly rulers or powers, neither present nor the future, neither the world above nor the world below, there is nothing in all creation that will be able to separate us from the love of God in Christ Jesus our Lord."

This is where we find our meaning. Think of the promise. Nothing in life or death, nothing in all creation, no illness, no event, nothing can separate us from the love of God. Nothing can stop us from being loved by God. It is to that love and mercy of God that we return to find the meaning of Mary's death. All other interpretations are beside the point. It is in the sure promise of a gracious and loving God where we find our meaning, our certainty, our hope.

Paul in his second letter to Timothy talks about his own coming death: *"I am already on the point of being sacrificed, the time of my departure has come. I have fought the good fight, I have finished the race, I have kept the faith. Henceforth, there is laid up for me the crown of righteousness, which the Lord will award to me on that day"* (2 Timothy 4:6-8).

The whole center of the Scriptures is found in the resurrection, Easter Sunday, and the promise which has been given again and again is that just as Jesus died and rose again, so also will we. There will be a new heaven and a new earth. There will be a new body like unto his glorious body. There will be a world where there is no more heartache, no more suffering, no more pain, no more illness, no more death. The Scriptures see death not as the end, but as a new beginning.

One final word. In 2 Corinthians 5:17 it is written, *"If anyone is in Christ, he or she is a new creation, the old has passed away, behold the new has come."* To be in Christ means that we are new people right now, we have eternal life right now, we are forgiven right now, we live in victory right now, we have the Holy Spirit right now. Too often we think this will happen only in the future, but if anyone is in Christ, he or she is a new creation right now.

The beauty and wonder of all of this is that for us who are today in that newness, this is not the final word. Rather we shall be reunited with Mary, with each other, with all the saints, in a world that goes far beyond what we could ever ask or think.

What a majestic promise that is and a promise that is intended for each of us.

DECISIONS AT THE TIME OF DEATH

*S*uddenly the unimaginable had become a reality. There is a death in the family. Either the death is imminent, or it has already happened. The survivors are gathered at the hospital, or in the home, or wherever the death may have taken place, and they are now wondering what decisions need to be made. There is a strong temptation to try and avoid making these decisions, to deny that such an event has happened, but there is an immediate need to take some specific actions. There is not the luxury of several days or weeks in which to deal with all of the issues.

Thus, it is important to know what decisions will have to be made at the time of a death. For the purposes of this book, we will center our discussion on three decisions. There may be more, but these are the essential decisions to be made right at the time of death.

1. Organ Donation

Today increasing numbers of people are finding new hope and health through the transplantation of vital organs and tissues. In fact, according to medical experts, there is no therapy or treatment which has had as dramatic an effect on illness as that of transplantation. Almost daily we hear aboust some of the miraculous gifts of life which take place, gifts of hearts and eyes and other vital organs.

Yet even though this new phenomenon has had a dramatic effect on the cure and care of those who are sick, many people wait in vain each year for necessary transplants. Many more people are in need than there are organs available. Much of this shortage is due to the fact that most people have not thought about this issue. We usually put off such decisions, thinking that we will probably live several more decades. There will be a time to consider such things, but it certainly is not now.

I hope this chapter will strongly encourage each of us to give consideration to this decisions, long before there is any death present in the family. It is not at all difficult to take the necessary steps to implement such a decision. Under the *Uniform Anatomical Gift Act*, all a person needs to do is sign a donor card, along with the signatures of two witnesses. There is a copy of this form at the end of this book. The basic guidelines of this Act of Congress include:

1. Any person 18 years of age or older can donate all or part of his or her body for transplantation, research, or placement in a tissue bank.

2. A donor's valid statement of a gift supercedes the rights of anyone else, unless a state autopsy prevails and has conflicting requirements.

3. If a donor has not acted in his lifetime to specify a wish to donate, his survivors may do so. The survivors are in specified order of priority: spouse, adult son or daughter, either parents, adult brother or sister, guardian, or any other person authorized or under obligation to dispose of the body.

4. Physicians who accept anatomical gifts, relying in good faith on documents provided to them in such cases, are protected from legal action.

5. Where a transplant is planned, the fact and time of death must be determined by a physician not involved in the transplant.

6. The donor has the right to revoke the gift, and it may be rejected by those for whom it is intended.

One of the advances of modern science is that many different parts of the body can be donated. For instance, eyes can be given to an eye bank for corneal transplants. This is the most successful kind of transplant and can restore sight to a blind person. Recently there was a published report about a woman who had been blind for 35 years, but with the reception of a corneal transplant, she saw her two daughters for the first time in her life.

It is important to make arrangements for donation of corneas beforehand, because the eyes must be removed within two to four hours after the death and must be carefully preserved. It is not possible in the case of the eyes to bequeath them to specific individuals; they will be used by the eye bank on the basis of a simple rotation. There are more than 60 eye banks in the United States, and people can check the local phone books for the address of the nearest one.

Ear bones can also be donated, and can be given to a temporal bone bank. These are used for research into ear disease and deafness. Again advance arrangements need to be made because removal of these bones is a difficult and specialized procedure. For further information one should contact the National Temporary Bone Banks Center (Baltimore, MD 21205) or the Deafness Research Foundation (336 Madison Avenue, New York, NY 10017).

Kidney transplants are also becoming more common, but there is still a serious shortage of kidneys for this purpose. More information may be secured through the National Kidney Foundation (116 East 27th Street, New York, NY 11010).

Pituitary glands are also used to produce growth hormones. An estimated five to ten thousand children in the country suffer from a major lack of this hormone, causing them to be abnormally short and limited in growth. It takes some 300 pituitary glands to provide enough growth hormone to allow one child to grow normally for a year. Therefore this treatment is available for only a small proportion of the children who can benefit from it. This work is coordinated by the National Pituitary Agency (Suite 503-7, 210 West Fayette Street, Baltimore, MD 21202).

Tissue transplant is also becoming much more common. More information can be gathered by contacting the Tissue Bank of the Naval Medical Research Institute (NNMC, Bethesda, MD 20014).

A coordinating group for much of the transplantation activity is called the Living Bank. This group works through the various transplant centers around the country. The Living Bank can be contacted at Box 6726 or 6631 Main Street, Houston, TX 77025. It has a 24-hour telephone service, 713-528-2971. The Bank will be happy to send out a Uniform Donor Card to keep in one's wallet and a Donor Registration form to return to the bank. The card will direct those who attend a gravely ill person to notify the bank immediately at the time of death.

There is no cost to the family of the deceased for removal of any organs or tissue. In addition, donation does not disfigure the body or affect the burial arrangements in any way. There may still be an open casket for reviewal if desired.

Organ donors should carry their donor card with them at all times. In many states it is now possible to indicate this willingness to donate on one's driver's license.

By way of summary, there are as many as 25 organs or tissues which can be transplanted. To give these organs at the time of death can be a very giving act, a commitment to helping others. However, it is far better to consider these decisions far in advance.

2. Donation of the Body for Research

It is also possible for a person to donate his or her body for the purposes of medical research. This can also be indicated on the donor card mentioned above. Again this can be a life-giving act, as thousands of bodies are needed each year to train future physicians and dentists.

The Uniform Gift Act was created to protect everyone concerned in this area of body donation. The basic intent of the act of Congress was that an individual should be able to control the disposition of his or her body after death, and the decisions made by this person should not be overruled by the next of kin. Thus, since 1968, all of the states have enacted laws which make it possible

for a person to give any part or all of the body for medical education, research, therapy or transplantation.

Individuals who wish to make such a donation should make
arrangements in advance with the medical school of their choice,
which will in turn supply the necessary forms. There will be one
copy which is kept by the school, and another copy should be
placed in the donor's important papers. The medical school may
also provide the donor with a uniform donor card, or some other
wallet-sized document, so that the school can be notified at the
time of death.

Prospective donors should carry these cards at all times. It is
also best if they inform their personal physician, lawyer, and family
members of this intention. Even though the anatomical gift law
gives a person the right to donate his or her body, many medical
schools require that the next of kin also give consent to the be-
quest after the death has occurred.

Whenever plans are made for the donation of one's body to a
medical school, alternative plans should be made for the disposition of the body, even though the medical school has accepted the
donation. There are also possible extenuating circumstances. For
instance, death may occur far away from the specific school, or in
areas where the medical school there may not need any more
bodies. Also, not all bodies are acceptable to the medical school.

Certain communicable diseases, such as meningitis or
hepatitis will disqualify this gift. Also, those bodies which have
been autopsied, had extensive surgery or were damaged seriously
in the death would not be acceptable. And bodies which are extremely obese, very emaciated or embalmed also are not taken.

When a donor dies, survivors should contact the anatomy
department of the medical school which was designated by the
deceased. If none was specified, then the anatomy department of the
nearest medical school should be contacted. Usually it is preferable
to have the body delivered to the medical school as soon as possible
after the death has occurred.

Most medical schools will pay for the transportation within
the state or within a certain radius. Others require the estate of the
deceased to pay any transportation costs, or to be covered by the

Social Security death benefit. If there is no surviving spouse, the medical school is legally entitled to recover this Social Security benefit to help cover the cost of the final disposition of the body. There also are instances where the medical school provides transportation or enlists an ambulance service.

When the research is completed, the final disposition of the body may be arranged in one of three ways.

1. The remains can be cremated and interred in a cemetery.
2. The remains can be cremated and returned to the family.
3. The remains can be returned to the family in a proper receptacle for burial in a cemetery.

3. Autopsy

There is one other way in which a person can give to others at the time of death. This is through an autopsy. An autopsy is an examination after death to determine the cause. It is required when the death results from anything other than natural causes, or if the cause is unknown. When the autopsy is required, there is no cost to the family. The results of the examination are then made known to the family verbally or by a letter but are not made public.

The major benefit of an autopsy is found in the assistance that it can give to medical science. It is able to extend the understanding and knowledge of science by the discovery of previously unsuspected diseases and causes of death. In addition, it can help to train medical personnel and to improve the standards of hospital care.

In a specific hospital, an autopsy can often help the staff to evaluate the diagnosis and treatment of that patient, and thus help in future treatment of illness. Of course there may be many times when an autopsy may produce no unexpected results. In some cases it may even be difficult to know with complete certainty the precise cause of death. However, in many situations the autopsy of the dead can serve to help the living.

To summarize, there are at least ten benefits which an autopsy can add to the preventative and curative aspects of medicine:

1. Determining the effectiveness of various treatments.
2. Detecting undesirable side-effects of various drugs.
3. Checking the failure or efficiency of surgical techniques.
4. Determining the cause of death for warning purposes
   (food poisoning, etc.).
5. Double checking the diagnosis.
6. Relieving family members of guilt.
7. Preventing legal problems.
8. Researching and understanding the disease, and discovering
   new diseases.
9. Identifying environmental factors and causes.
10. Supplying genetic disease information for the family.

A word of caution should also be raised about autopsies. If the autopsy is not required, the cost can range from $750 to $1,200. This cost is often borne by the hospital, but not always. It would be wise for the family to check on any responsibility for this cost before giving authorization. Written consent of the next of kin is necessary before an autopsy will be done, unless one is required.

In most cases an autopsy will not disfigure a body for reviewal, but it could be a factor in some cases. An autopsy can also be included on a uniform donor card.

In essence, these decisions to be made at the time of death often are not that difficult to make. This chapter might be dismissed in just a few seconds by those who must make these decisions. However, if there has been no prior communication between members of the family about such issues, such decisions can be wrenching. Family members should all be very clear about what decisions will be made long before the need arises. There is nothing like being prepared to make the moment of death less painful for the survivors.

FUNERALS

*I*mmediately upon the death of a loved one, the family must turn its attention to the planning of a funeral. A wide variety of decisions can be made, and the chapter that follows this one will explain some of these options. However, it might be helpful to describe an overview of the development of the funeral, and how we have come to this point.

Funerals have changed dramatically in the past century. We may assume that we are carrying on some great Judeo-Christian tradition, burying our dead in the way we do, but the tradition we've developed has little or nothing to do with funerals of prior historical periods. This is not to say that the way we organize and handle funerals today is necessarily wrong, although some would certainly make that claim, but it is to say that we have no historical precedent to give us an assurance that we are standing in some great tradition of the ages.

Up until the 19th century, funerals were primarily the responsibility of the family, the friends and the church. There were no funeral homes or undertakers. Death was seen more as a natural part of life and a part of a family's caretaking for its own. The whole event of the funeral, the disposition of the body and the caring for the survivors was an action of the larger community. The only outside help sometimes secured was that of a town carpenter, who was asked to construct a simple wooden coffin. However, it was also common for a member of the family or a friend or neighbor to build the coffin.

The term "undertaker" did not originate until some people in the 19th century "undertook" to provide assistance on a more regular basis to those who experienced death, and also at this time began to handle the body. Morticians basically came about during the Civil War when the need suddenly arose to preserve the bodies of the soldiers killed in battle in order to ship them long distances for burial. Thus, it wasn't until the latter part of the 19th century that more elaborate funeral practices and the funeral director present today had their beginnings. Only in recent years has the funeral home evolved to its current status of providing a place for the preparation of the body and the possibility of visitation and a service.

By way of example, the book *Foxfire* captures some of the flavor of funerals before our more modern approach came to be. As soon as a person died in the latter part of the 19th century and the early part of the 20th, the whole community would rally around the grieving family. Bells were tolled from the local church, announcing the death to all those persons who were within hearing distance. Neighbors often gathered to construct the coffin, unless it had been built in advance, perhaps even under the supervision of the person who had died. There was no attempt to hide the reality of what had happened. Denial was not a factor. Relatives were notified as soon as a death took place, sometimes by means of a letter edged in a black border.

Because the body could not be preserved for any length of time, it was important that the service and burial be held at the earliest possible moment. The body was washed and dressed in the family home and furnished with the best clothes the family owned. If there was no appropriate clothing which could be used, the neighbors would furnish what was needed. The caring community would gather with those in mourning, and some close friends would even spend the night so that the survivors did not have to stay alone.

The funeral service was usually very simple, lasting between a half-hour and an hour. Digging and filling the grave was a sacred act which was often reserved for friends and relatives. They would all make a link around the grave, forming a human chain. One person would begin by saying the words, "Ashes to ashes, dust to dust," and then throw one shovelful of dirt. This would continue until the coffin was completed covered. After the funeral and the burial, people from the community would stay with the family for a day or two. Later, a rather simple and crude tombstone would be placed over the grave. This too was provided by the community, free of charge.

There was a descriptive narrative in the book, *Foxfire*, by a Dr. Rufas Morgan, a retired 80-year-old Episcopalian minister from Franklin, North Carolina. Here are some of his words:

I really wish that the same burial customs that used to be present were still here. There wasn't any idea of a metal casket or a means of preserving the remains. Rather we lived what the Scriptures say, *"Dust thou art and unto dust thou shall return."* And I would much rather think of my body going back to the earth where it came from and fertilizing some tree or grass or flower, than just having a metal box with me inside preserved like a mummy.

We have gotten away from the wagon now, we have a hearse and a funeral home. Instead of the neighbors coming into the house and comforting the mourners, they go to the funeral home the night before the funeral.

Another change I have noticed is a distortion of emphasis. We have made flowers to be the center of the visitation. Everything is all dollied up to pretend that a death has not really happened. When I die, I want the money to be spent for something to carry out some ministry or charity, not to spend it on flowers. If the flowers are in bloom outside, and I love wildflowers, I'd like for the children or somebody I've known to pick some of these flowers along the way as they come to the funeral. If the wildflowers aren't in bloom, then sprays from the hemlock trees or the balsam or pine.

In the way of music, I don't want any mournful songs sung at my funeral. St. Paul says, *"Be not sorry for those who have departed."* A Christian has hope and looks forward to being with Christ. The faithful servant lives on. When I die I want Easter hymns sung at my funeral because they are so joyful. They are hopeful. They reflect our belief in the resurrection of the dead.

Thus says Dr. Morgan.

While we recognize how different funerals were in the recent, and also in the distant past, we also know that there is probably no turning back from where we are today. Any challenge to the practices of today is difficult; in fact, there is a good pressure to accept things just the way they are. It is important, however, that we look carefully at the way we treat our dead and the way we plan and implement funerals.

If there are aspects of the present customs that we do not like, then we should not be afraid to change them. This should be one of the most important roles of a congregation, to study the issues surrounding death and dying and to help people know what decisions to make. It is important that we be intentional about what we decide, rather than just accepting the prevailing cultural customs.

Funeral procedures and understandings are also in a process of evolution. One of the most obvious changes in recent years has to do with funeral directors. In the past they were seen primarily as undertakers, morticians who were called to take care of the body. Now they are attempting to move beyond this role of just providing goods and services and arranging for the disposition of the body.

Now the aim among many is to make the funeral director into a professional person, to make his career one of high calling. Many funeral directors today refer to themselves as grief therapists who have some special therapeutic function in caring for the bereaved, in addition to taking care of the deceased. Whether this becomes accepted by the larger public remains to be seen, but it certainly is a trend, as we turn more and more of the responsibilities surrounding death over to others.

In keeping with this development, the licensing requirements for funeral directors are increasing. In most states the funeral directors must be licensed, especially those who do embalming. The requirements for this license include, at the minimum, a high school degree, and often some additional schooling. Some states have begun to require that funeral directors have at least one or two years of college education, including a period of internship lasting a year or more, followed by a state board licensing examination. At the present time there is much diversity in the educational backgrounds of funeral directors.

Lay people should understand something about the funeral director because, at the time of a death, he or she stands in forefront of most decision making. Rarely does anyone arrange for a funeral anymore without contacting a funeral director. But the funeral director stands alone, or perhaps together with the pastor, as the the key player In the funeral planning and implementation. More details will be forthcoming in chapter ten.

Most persons who deal with the funeral director are completely unprepared to do so. There is probably no event in our life for which we have less awareness or understanding; thus, it can be an especially traumatic and unsettling time. In addition, because we are not prepared, it also means that we might make some decisions which are not in the best interests of the deceased, the surviving family, or the surrounding community. The *Consumer's Union Report* suggests five reasons why this contact with the funeral director can be so difficult.

1. Emotional Trauma

All studies show that shock is the first response to the death of an important person in our lives. This shock affects the whole system. Survivors are filled with confusion and disorientation. therefore, during the first day or two after such a death, grieving persons are usually not able to come to grips with what has taken place. Yet it is at this very time that they are asked to make funeral decisions, many of which involve substantial sums of money.

2. Guilt

Most survivors are caught up in the "if onlys" — if only we would have said something, or not said something. Guilt is right up there near the top of the emotions we experience at the time of death. Thus, it is not unusual for people to want to alleviate that guilt, to make it up to the deceased. The only way that seems to be left is through some kind of elaborate funeral. At the same time guilt can often lead a family to try to impress a wider community by the expensive funeral. "We really did love this person; let us show everyone how much." Guilt should not influence the decisions that people make, but when they are not prepared ahead of time, it is usually an influential factor.

3. Dependency and Suggestibility

It is a fact of grieving that survivors are very often unable to make decisions; there is a time of numbness, of paralysis. Thus, they are often looking to others to help make decisions for them. Widows and widowers often look to their immediate families for assistance. "Tell me what I should do," they plead. However, it is also common for the grieving persons to transfer this dependency to the funeral director. After all, this person is obviously an expert, so this next step becomes, "Tell me what to do. What is the best decision to make? What is appropriate?" However, this is not a wise way to make what should be informed business decisions.

4. Lack of Knowledge

In ordinary situations of life, consumers have much available information and have usually been able to do some comparison pricing. In the case of a funeral, however, this may be the first time a person has ever encountered such an experience. The person is completely in the dark about what is needed, what is proper, and what the costs should be. It is hard to imagine anyone more vulnerable than someone in this kind of situation.

5. Time Pressure

In most situations in which we are making major purchases, we ahve some time to consider, to ponder and then decide. At least we should. After a death, however, there is a severe lack of time available for decisions, such as removing the body and planning the funeral, decisions which must be made promptly. This extreme pressure to act immediately often increases a person's dependence on the advice and counsel of the funeral director.

It also limits a person's ability to obtain adequate information and to make an informed business decision.

All of the dynamics listed above can cause survivors to be very helpless and defenseless when meeting with the funeral director. Even if a whole family goes along to this meeting, the grief and stress may be of such a level that good judgment is not possible. This is not to say that most funeral directors are dishonest or are deliberately trying to take advantage of people. In fact, my own impression is that the overwhelming majority of them are persons of integrity.

At the same time, they are in the business to make a profit, to sell certain goods and services, which is a very American thing to do. In order to make this profit, therefore, they are going to suggest and encourage those who come to purchase certain available commodities. There is nothing wrong with this; we just need to be completely aware of this situation. It also is the American way to not spend money that we do not need to spend, to be frugal, to find a less expensive alternative, if this is our wish. We should not apologize for this decision.

I would strongly encourage that when survivors go to the funeral home to make the necessary decisions, they bring with them a family friend for assistance and support. It would be preferable to bring someone who has made such arrangements before and who knows something of the financial situation of the family. When appropriate, it is usually helpful to have a member of the clergy present. Whoever accompanies the family to the funeral home should be an advocate, one who can help the grieving persons to ask the right questions and to be less vulnerable to the various kinds of pressure that are at work.

I also recommend that when survivors meet with the funeral director, they get as much in writing as possible, including all price information. This should be done before any other matters are discussed, examining all the goods and services which are available, along with the costs. It is also important that survivors not disclose to the funeral director how much money is available for the funeral, either in death benefits, life insurance or cash.

Obviously, the funeral director is well aware of the compensation which comes from Social Security and veteran's benefits, but it is best not to reveal too much. Morticians are certainly entitled to know that they will be paid promptly for their goods and services, and they want a definite understanding of the payment schedule. However, people can protect themselves from greater costs by not revealing the amount of money they have for a funeral.

The *Consumers Union* suggests that the written price list is crucial. This list should include all costs, including those at the cemetery. This will make it possible for the family to give the funeral director a price range for the total cost. The experience of many is that if the detailed price list is not provided before the purchase, the final bill is often much higher than expected or anticipated.

This may all sound obvious; it is the way just about every other business operates. However, many funeral homes only print the names of the specific goods and services. The prices are written in by the director at the time of the meeting with the family, or more likely, at a later time when the family is not present. This often creates a situation where there is no standard price. The funeral director simply charges what he believes the traffic will bear. Price itemization is the best protection for any family making funeral arrangements.

There are basically two ways to finance a funeral. Very few persons will pay the full amount at the time of the first meeting. However, many funeral directors will give cash discounts if the bills are paid promptly. Rather, the majority ask the customer to sign an agreement or contract that may carry no finance charges for the first three or four months. After that, interest is most often charged.

This delay in payment recognizes that it often takes some time to process and collect the Social Security and veteran's benefits, as well as those life insurance or pension benefits. The delay also is an indicator that the settlement of an estate may take much longer. Most funeral homes offer installment plans, with a fixed amount to be paid weekly or monthly.

6. Benefits

There is a lump-sum payment of $300 in 1987 for those buried at a national cemetery and up to $450 for those who use a private cemetery. Claims must be filed either by the survivor of the veteran's family or a non-relative who can present proof of payment for a veteran's funeral arrangements. A funeral director may also be authorized to file this claim. It must be filed within two years of the time of death.

The documents necessary to file this claim include:

1. Veteran's discharge papers
2. Certified copy of the death certificate.
3. Copy of the marriage certificate, where applicable.
4. Receipted itemized bill from a funeral home.

All claims must be made on authorized forms from the Veteran's Administration. In addition to the lump-sum payment, other available benefits include an American flag for the casket, a burial plot in the nearest Veteran's cemetery or a $150 payment if burial is in a private cemetery, and a suitable bronze or granite memorial tablet or marker.

A veteran who dies of military-service-related disabilities receives a total of approximately $1100 in death benefits, plus free burial in a national cemetery, a headstone and flag.

The spouse and any minor child of a veteran are also entitled to free burial in a national cemetery. If the spouse or minor child of the veteran dies first, he or she may be buried in a national cemetery, if the veteran signs a paper confirming intent to be buried next to the deceased.

If the veteran dies first and is buried in a private cemetery, the spouse and minor child of the veteran no longer have the right to be buried in a national cemetery. Application for burial in a national cemetery should be made at the time of death for the veteran, or of an eligible dependent, by applying to the superintendent of the nearest cemetery in which burial is desired.

All veterans are entitled to headstones and the U.S. flag. In some cases, transportation costs for the remains are paid by the Veteran's Administration. If a veteran dies in a VA facility where he or she was properly admitted for hospital, nursing home or domicile care, the VA is usually required to pay the cost of transporting the body to the place of burial. The same benfit applies when the veteran dies en route while traveling under the authorization of the VA for the pur-pose of examination, treatment or care.

Under certain circumstances, members of the National Guard, Armed Forces Reserves, and Reserve Officers Training Corps (ROTC) also qualify for death benefits.

Whether survivors prefer to apply for death benefits themselves or use the services of a funeral director, they will need copies of a number of documents and personal and business papers in order to prove death and receive benefits. Survivors will need the following:

1. At least ten certified copies of the death certificate to establish insurance claims. These will be needed for Social Security and VA benefits as well as other claims.
2. Copies of birth certificates of the surviving spouse and minor children for Social Security and VA benefits.
3. Copies of the marriage certificate for Social Security and VA benefits for the surviving spouse and minor children.
4. Copy of the of the W-2 form or federal income tax return for the most recent calendar year as proof of the decedent's employment record for Social Security benefits.
5. Copy of the veteran's discharge papers for VA benefits.
6. Copy of a receipted bill from the funeral home for VA benefits, also for Social Security benefits if the applicant is not the surviving spouse.

Survivors should know the Social Security number of the deceased to claim these benefits. In addition to these documents listed above, survivors should locate important papers such as the following:

1. Bankbooks.
2. Stock certificates.
3. Real estate deeds and mortgages.
4. Credit card bills.
5. Installment loan and service contracts.
6. Life insurance and mortgage policies.

Survivors should also contact organizations and institutions the deceased worked for, belonged to, or had business dealings with, reporting the death and requesting information about any life or health insurance policies, special funds, or pensions to which the survivors might be entitled.

Social Security Benefits

At the time of death, there is a maximum lump-sum payment of $255. This is given to the widow or widower, if living together with the deceased at the time of death. If there is no surviving spouse eligible for payment, it may be paid to the person who pays the funeral expenses.

Every person who has worked under Social Security for ten years or for one and one-half years during the three years prior to death, is normally eligible for the benefit. Applications for benefits must be filed within two years of the date of death. It is desirable to file the claim immediately after the death.

The documents needed to support a claim for Social Security death benefits include:

1. Employment record of the deceased for the most recent calendar year (W-2 form).
2. Birth certificates of minor children.
3. Birth certificate of widow or widower if age 60 or above; if disabled, then 50 or above.
4. Copy of marriage certificate (only with application for widow's monthly payment).

Proof of a decedent's death may also be required, together with a Social Security card or record of that number, and a receipted funeral bill.

If there are any expenses related to the donating of the body to a medical facility, Social Security will reimburse these costs, although this sum will probably not be the full $255.

Other Benefits

1. If the death arises out of an accident in the course of employment, there may be Workman's Compensation Insurance Benefits.
2. Federal, state and some local governments award survivors' benefits to families of some of their civilian employees.

3. A number of states which have no-fault automobile insurance will issue payment to cover funeral and burial expenses for someone killed in a motor vehicle accident. The survivors of a person killed in Minnesota could receive $2000 or more, depending on a number of conditions.

In summary, it is most helpful to gather all the information possible ahead of time. People who are not in a death situation can meet with a local funeral director, or more than one director, to gain more understanding about the whole decision-making process. The best time to discuss funeral planning, as well as the costs that would be incurred, is when a limited amount of emotion is present.

It would be a perfect time to walk through the casket room, if there is one in that funeral home, and to look at the price itemization list. Funeral directors almost without exception are more than pleased to visit with a prospective buyer and to show the variety of goods and services which are available. To make some or all of these decisions ahead of time would avoid many of the pitfalls detailed in this chapter.

DECISIONS BEFORE CALLING A FUNERAL DIRECTOR

A death has just occurred. The family is gathered together either at the place of death or in their home. The decisions about organ donation and autopsy have been made. Now it is essential to think about the next few days, about further decisions to be made, and about the funeral.

There is often a sense of unreality about these moments. Most of those present would rather leave these decisions for another time. Perhaps with time everything about this event will go away and the nightmare will be over. Denial is never too far away at the time of death. In spite of these feelings which may be present, there are decisions that need to be made, and the best time to do this is right away, before a funeral director is contacted. A pastor is also available to be with the family at this time and should be consulted.

There are at least nine major decisions that need to be made when a death has occurred. Some of these may be easy; others may be more difficult.

1. Will there be a "traditional" funeral, or will some very different arrangements be made?

The conventional American funeral has an understandable, acceptable way of proceeding, and the majority of people will feel comfortable choosing this path. It involves the traditional activities of choosing a casket, arranging for a visitation, planning a funeral service and making arrangements for a burial. There are certainly many options within this framework, but there are some specific parameters as well.

However, there are also some alternatives which would be a substantial variation from the usual. It may be that there is an immediate cremation, or that the body is donated to medical science. Possibly, some might avoid the funeral home altogether. There certainly are options that are not mentioned in this book.

As a practical matter, if an individual or a family has not done some planning ahead of time, an alternative most likely cannot be pursued at the time of death. There is more than a little inherent pressure on surviving families to follow the traditional route. However, for those who haven't yet lost a family member, there are other alternatives to consider. These are certainly consistent with our Christian values and may have strong meaning for some families.

In essence, I would strongly encourage families to talk about these issues long before a death is imminent. Funeral arrangements are far less painful to make when a family has faced this issue in advance. But, if this is the first time such a discussion has taken place, then it can be incredibly difficult.

2. If there is to be a casket, will it be open or closed?

This is probably the most important decision in the whole funeral process, for this will determine much of what happens, as well as the cost. There are some persuasive arguments on either side of this issue, and this book will not attempt to make a final judgment. Again, it is better if the decision is made in advance.

One school of thought claims emphatically that the survivors benefit both emotionally and psychologically from viewing the dead. Seeing helps a person to believe, they say. It is a way of dealing intentionally with the reality of death.

Psychologist Ann Kilima, as quoted in the *Consumer's Union Report*, suggests that viewing the body is a crucial factor in beginning the process of mourning. Viewing provides the opportunity to accept the fact of death and to say the last good-byes to the deceased. She also contends that children are aided by this viewing, for it tends to counter their inclination to indulge in a great deal of fantasy and magical thinking. She says that the reality of the open casket is often less frightening than their misconceptions about death. In the case of viewing, however, the children should be prepared ahead of time for what to expect at a reviewal.

Another school says just the opposite. By concentrating on a cosmetically made-up body that appears to be just resting or sleeping, survivors are helped to deny the reality of death. Dr. Avery Wiseman of the Harvard Medical School, in the same article mentioned above, says that there is no evidence that viewing is necessary to begin the grief process. Grief and bereavement are complicated individual processes and cannot be so easily categorized. More important than the event of viewing, he suggests, is the quality of the support system.

Both sides make persuasive arguments, and each family needs to weigh this decision carefully. However, I think also that we can make a distinction between a sudden, unexpected death and that which takes place after a long and lingering illness. If a person dies suddenly and without warning, it is extremely difficult for the survivors to believe that this has happened. Sometimes in such a situation, viewing can be helpful. Of course, the best time for viewing is by the bedside at the time of death. This is far more real than after embalming has taken place. Of course, this kind of viewing is not always possible, especially in the case of accidents, or where family members are separated by long distances.

However, if a person has been failing over a period of time, if there has been a terminal illness present or just the natural results of old age, then viewing may not be as important. In effect, family members may have already started grief work long before the actual death takes place. They may have seen the process of dying through all the stages.

One more comment should be made. There is, in my judgment, no psychological or emotional need for the viewing of the body by anyone outside of the immediate family and closest friends. Casual friends or neighbors do not need a reviewal to deal with grief; it is done often more out of curiosity than for therapeutic reasons. Often foremost in their conversation is the funeral director's skill, or lack of it, rather than any grief work.

To view the body or not to view. That is a crucial question at the time of death. It is a decision best made in advance.

3. Will there be a funeral service or a memorial service?

By way of distinction, a funeral service has the body present; a memorial service is without the casket. This is the only real difference. In the event of a memorial service, a number of factors may have brought this about. The burial may have taken place at an earlier time. There may have been a cremation or body donation to a medical school. The body may be missing for some reason, as in the case of drowning or of an air disaster.

From a Christian perspective, there is no one way which is preferable. Either a memorial service or a funeral service is perfectly appropriate, and both can be a wonderful testimony to the Easter message of Christ.

4. Where and when should the service take place?

A Christian funeral or memorial service is best held in the church. It is not the only place for such a service, but it is the best place. For the Christian church is where so many of our most significant life experiences have occurred: baptism, confirmation, reception of the Lord's Supper, responding to the proclamation of the Word of God, perhaps a wedding, and many, many times of closeness with other Christians. A part of a rich tradition is to return to this place of meaning, promise and love.

In addition, the church is that place which contains so many important symbols of our faith: the cross, the altar, the baptismal font, the liturgy, the hymns of faith. It is the house of prayer, the worship center, and the place where the Christian community can gather so naturally to celebrate God's grace in Jesus Christ and to express our deep love and caring as others are hurting.

From the standpoint of the church itself, I believe there should be no financial charge for the use of the church at the time of a funeral. It is one of our most important ministries, and there should be no barriers placed in the way. Also, I believe we should be open to the funeral service of anyone who makes such a request.

There are many churches which put up restrictions, who keep certain people out, those who are not members, those who have committed suicide, or those who have not demonstrated sufficient religious zeal. I believe that to prohibit people from a funeral service in the church is a tragic misuse of the Gospel.

Times arise when we need to take a firm stand, to stick to our values. I think that weddings may be a time to do this, but not the time of death. A funeral is one of the finest opportunities we have to proclaim the Gospel of Jesus Christ. How can we possibly turn down such an open door for ministry? Also, we need to remember more unchurched people are probably present at a funeral than are present in our sanctuaries the rest of the year.

What a time to witness to the resurrection! What a time to proclaim the grace and love of God! We who follow Christ need to always remember his words, *"Come unto me all who are weary and burdened, and I will give you rest" (Matthew 11:28).*

Sometimes it may be more appropriate to have the service in a funeral home or some other location. This is also perfectly consistent with the Christian faith, and such a service can also be the occasion for the celebration of victory and resurrection.

5. What time should be set for the service?

A funeral or memorial service should be scheduled primarily for the convenience of loved ones and friends. This will vary depending on the specific situation. Usually this service will take place three or four days following the death, although there are certainly exceptions to this time frame. It is best not to have the service too soon or to rush the events. On the other hand, it is also important not to delay the time of the service for too long.

Funeral and memorial services most often have been held during the daytime hours. This has been especially true in those communities where it is relatively easy for people to be absent from work in order to attend. A daytime service is usually held in the late morning or the early afternoon. It is most convenient if there are many who drive from a distance, especially those who elderly, for it gives them an opportunity to return home in daylight. There is also ample time for a burial if it occurs nearby, and time to return to the church for a reception.

In recent years, an increasing number of services have been held in the evening. This is particularly the case where it is not convenient for people to attend during the day. An evening service often allows some to attend who could not otherwise do so. In our own experience, the crowds at a service in the evening are usually considerably larger than those in the daytime. However, if there is to be a burial, this generally cannot occur at night, thus it must take place either prior to the service or the following day.

It is important that these decisions of time and place be fully coordinated with the pastor. The use of the church building always involves a consideration of schedules, as well as the availability of both the pastor and the funeral director.

6. If there is a burial, where will it take place?

Surprisingly enough, this is often one of the most difficult of the decisions to be made, if it has not already been made. More people have made this choice than most others surrounding a death. But when the decision has not been made in advance, it means quite often that the survivors are not only planning the palce of burial for the loved one, they are also making some determinations of burial for themselves. This can be very sobering, and can bring people face to face with the fact of their own mortality.

A place of burial is influenced by many different considerations. Family history, geography, religious tradition and convenience for the living all play a part in this decision. Generally speaking, cemetery space in urban and suburban areas is increasing in cost at a rather substantial rate, and can be quite costly. Cemeteries in more rural areas are usually less expensive. More specific information is contained in Chapter 12.

7. What general dollar amount will be the limit for spending, and from where will this money come?

As was mentioned before, an almost unlimited amount may be spent on a funeral. Quite probably a family will spend more than they wish to spend. However, before the funeral director is contacted the family should have some basic agreement on how much is enough and from what sources the money will come. This will make it much easier to choose the various options available.

8. Will there be a memorial fund?

Many churches set up memorial funds for those members who die and encourage people to contribute to this fund. After the money is received, most churches will ask the family to designate where this memorial fund might be used. At this time the church can list some specific needs that the family might wish to address.

A wide variety of other charities might be designated as the recipients of memorial money. It is best to indicate this decision in the obituary notice, so that people can plan and act accordingly.

9. What funeral home should be contacted?

If desired, the funeral home will take over after the previous questions have been answered and make most of the arrangements. It would certainly be advantageous if the family had been in that funeral home before, so that there was some basic awareness of the facility and procedures. It would also be best if the family could ask someone who had used the funeral home in the past about this experience, that way discovering the positives and negatives. This would make for a more informed decision.

Usually, a pastor can give some information about one or more funeral homes in the area and, if asked, could share some strengths and weaknesses about these businesses. However, the pastor should be careful not to recommend any specific home, but to rather present the options which are available.

Even though it is not the ideal situation, the first time the funeral director normally meets a family is when he goes to pick up the body, or at an appointed time at the funeral home. At this time it is very difficult to change funeral homes.

In summary, it is best to make the decisions discussed above as soon after the death of a loved one as possible. Numbers one through eight ideally should be made before contacting a funeral director. If this is done, then the necessary arrangements should be easier to make. The emotional and psychological pressure to make impulsive decisions would be lessened. This should be the goal of all of us who wish to protect and take care of our families.

CASKETS

*T*here are many decisions which need to be made which have a strong impact on the overall cost of a funeral, but there is no more important choice than that of the casket. Some funerals will not have caskets, but in the majority which do, this is the single most influential element in the cost and shape of the funeral.

1. Costs in General

Cost should not be the only determinative factor in the funeral planning. There are many other important considerations. However, no matter in what direction the funeral might go, the funeral buyer must be as aware as possible of all of the costs and options. Much of the following material has been gleaned from a thorough study of the funeral industry entitled *Funerals: Consumers' Last Rights*, an excellent resource issued by the *Consumer's Union Report* in 1977. Some of the material is now outdated, but it nevertheless gives a complete picture of the major issues which all funeral buyers need to confront.

Back at the end of the 19th century, when furniture dealers were then the retail suppliers of caskets, they established a consistent method of pricing. Casket makers advised these dealers to charge three times the wholesale cost of the casket, to recover the cost of the casket, to cover overhead, and to make a profit. This means that caskets cost the consumer three times what they cost the seller.

In the 20th century, with the rapid growth of urban society, many changes have occurred. Funeral homes have become more important as private homes have become smaller, and as apartments have become more common. Visitations have gravitated to that place having more room. In addition, undertaking has taken on more services, such as embalming. The job of a funeral director has become a full-time occupation. Thus the overhead went up, and so the old markup value of the casket changed. The ratio of three to one became four to one, or five to one, depending on the costs of that particular home.

Today the multiple of five to one remains a reasonably accurate index. Now, with such a system in place it makes all sorts of sense for the funeral director to try and sell higher-priced caskets. The greater the cost of the casket, obviously, the more substantial the profit.

One problem in the pricing of funerals is the wide range of ways costs are determined. Caskets fall under several different pricing systems:

A. Unit Pricing

In this system, the price that is listed on the casket represents the cost for the "complete" funeral. In other words, what you pay for the casket is supposed to include all the costs for goods and services. However, this price tag can be misleading, for in a large percentage of situations, the complete funeral is anything but complete. It may include the basic and standard items, but does not usually provide for any extras, which can be defined any way the funeral director wishes to do so.

B. Bi-Unit Pricing

This is a service-charge method, which separates the merchandise from the service. There is one price for the casket and a separate price for the various services provided by the funeral director. This form of pricing originated because many buyers believed they were paying too much for caskets under the unit pricing system.

C. Functional Pricing

This separates the pricing into even more specific areas. The price of the casket is separate. A second category would be the professional and staff services, and a third includes the funeral home and facilities. There can also be an additional component which covers the special automobiles which are used.

D. Price Itemization

This is simply the method by which each item and service offered in a funeral is given a specific price. The major advantage to the buyer is that what is being purchased is quite clearly listed. It is also easier in this system to reject any items which are not wanted, and thus reduce the overall cost of the funeral. On the surface, this is probably the best alternative.

However, it is important to know that this last alternative does not always offer the protection it might suggest. If the buyer rejects certain items or services, the funeral dirctor may still arbitrarily raise the prices of other items in order to compensate. This is especially true where the price itemization lists do not include the prices, but are written in by the funeral director. This can give carte blanche to the funeral director to chage whatever he feels the traffic might bear. The consumer has almost no way of knowing if the price being charged is the same price that is charged to others.

To restate some important recommendations from previous chapters, the buyers should always get as much in writing as is possible before many any decisions about the purchase of a casket. It is preferable to have a complete price information sheet, with all of the prices listed, so that only those items will be purchased which are truly wanted, at a price which seems reasonable and affordable. To have all of this information written in a clear and concise manner will eliminate most of the surprises which have a habit of appearing in many funeral bills.

2. The Selection Room

For those who have never gone through the process of a casket selection, the description which follows may seem so unbelievable and bizarre you may think that it is just a funny caricature, or that we must be talking about another period of history. But be assured that this is startlingly real, and that it can be more than a little disturbing to those who must go through with it. For anyone who has made funeral arrangements some of this may sound familiar, although most persons who have gone through such an experience are completely unaware of the dynamics which were present in that situation. What we are describing is the selection room.

The selection room is the most important aspect of the funeral director's business. It has not been left to chance. Here is where the greatest potential for profit is found, and it is also here where the funeral director could quickly move into bankruptcy. Therefore, great care is taken to arrange the caskets in this room, and often no cost is spared to reach the desired effect. All of this is done to apply the maximum amount of psychological pressure to the buyer in hopes that a significant amount of money might be spent.

Consider for a moment the setting in the typical selection room. It usually has a great deal of spaciousness. (The recommended amount is at least 40 square feet per casket.) There is most likely wall-to-wall carpeting, done in a soft color to enhance the room's atmosphere. Lighting is done with extreme care. It is planned so that all shadows might be avoided, and the luster and polish of the caskets might be enhanced. This is all designed with complete intentionality.

For those who might question this description, it is helpful to consider the advice of Wilber Krieger of the National Morticians in his book *Successful Funeral Service Management*. He sets forth the classic plan for selling high-priced caskets, and according to the Federal Trade Commission, his advice is still highly recommended in trade manuals for funeral directors. In other words, most funeral homes in this country still follow his basic plan.

He constructed a system that is based on the price range that the funeral director would prefer people to buy. The major goal is to sell the greatest number of caskets at a price just above the median. Therefore, the largest group of caskets which are displayed should fall somewhere in this price range.

For instance, notes Krieger, if there are 30 caskets in the selection room, three should be in the lowest price area, eight in the next, 12 in the group just above the median, and seven in the highest. As a rule, most funeral directors do not expect to sell the highest priced caskets, but the more of these high price caskets which are present, the higher the median is likely to be.

Krieger draws a picture of the arrangement of the selection room. When you first enter, the first casket you should see is one of very high price. This may shock the buyer, and he will quickly turn to the one nearby. This is often the least expensive and certainly looks like it. The buyer now will often be repulsed and does not want to consider something so gaudy. The next caskets to be viewed will then be those priced just above the median, the ones the funeral director really wants to sell. Usually the selection room will not contain very many low priced caskets, for that makes it too easy to buy one in this range. According to the *Consumer's Union*, if a low priced casket sells too well, it is usually removed.

In addition, according to the Federal Trade Commission, there is much evidence to suggest that funeral directors or casket manufacturers deliberately vulgarize the less expensive caskets. Poor finishing, use of tawdry lining material, or a fabric of garish colors is quite common. It is not unusual that inexpensive caskets will be colored somewhere between a lavender or pink, which is often quite effective in discouraging potential buyers away from this choice.

The funeral director wishes to paint a picture of a pressure-less experience in the picking of a casket. He or she may not even be in the room with the survivors, merely suggesting that they look and discuss things on their own. But the design of the room is meant to sell higher priced caskets.

It certainly can be argued that there is nothing wrong with it; it is the American way. Car dealers, furniture salesmen, real estate agents, and many others are realistically trying to sell more expensive models. That is certainly legitimate. However, it is also okay if we are aware of all of this and enter such a situation with enough knowledge and tools to make the kind of decisions we really wish to make. It is just as American for the consumer to try and spend less money as it is for the funeral director to sell higher priced goods.

Not all funeral homes have a casket selection room on the premises. Customers at some homes can choose from a catalog, from photographs or slides, or even visit a nearby wholesaler. In general, these funeral homes tend to have much lower average prices than those with selection rooms.

It is also possible even in funeral homes which have a selection room to choose a casket from a catalog or pictorial display, if the consumer requests it. This would tend to avoid much of the pressure some people feel when looking at the actual models. A customer may also ask to see caskets which are not available in the selection room, either at a wholesaler or in a catalog.

Types of Caskets

There are three main types of caskets:

1. A full couch, in which the entire body can be viewed.
2. A half couch, which shows the body from the waist up. This is the most common casket chosen.
3. Casket with a lift, a removable cover. This is found only on the most inexpensive models.

There is a considerable range of material used in constructing coffins. The less expensive woods — such as pine, chestnut, cypress, red cedar — are usually covered with cloth. The more expensive hardwoods — such as oak, birch, maple, cherry, mahogany — are treated with clear natural finishes. Metal is still another material very common in the manufacture of caskets, as well as other specially treated iron, steel, copper and bronze.

According to *Consumer's Union*, about 67% of all caskets are made of steel, while 15 to 16% are hardwoods. About 13% are covered with cloth. Steel has grown in popularity in recent years because buyers have accepted the claim that it will do a better job in preserving the body. There is no evidence that any casket will preserve the body, and the reason why anyone should try and do this is obscure. However, this is a common reason why people will buy a more expensive and well-constructed casket.

As one purchases goods and services from a funeral director, it is also helpful to remember the Code of Professional Responsibilities of the National Funeral Directors Association: "The director shall provide the necessary services and merchandise in keeping with the wishes and finances of the family or their representatives."

In addition, it is instructive to know about the Code of Good Practices which is accepted by the National Selected Morticians who promise: "To assure each purchaser complete freedom to exercise his preference in selecting a funeral service within his means."

The purpose of this chapter is simply to take the funeral directors at their word and exercise one's complete freedom.

4. Specific Costs

A funeral home in our area has the following prices for a funeral in 1987, etc.

Standard service charge $1695
This includes:
Professional services 655
Embalming 270
Cosmetology and body preparation 80
Use of facility..239
Visitation 95
Funeral Service 80
Transfer of body..80
Funeral coach 105
Lead car/Utility van, flowers 50
Register book..6
Thank you cards...5
Service folders 30

Caskets ....From $535 to $4735
Concrete liner or vault ....From $400 to $1675

The average cost per funeral is $3,000 to $4,000. This cost *does not* include burial costs.

It is obvious that the above costs may not reflect the costs in many communities throughout the country; prices may be higher

The average cost per funeral is $3,000 to $4,000. This cost *does not* include burial costs.

It is obvious that the above costs may not reflect the costs in many communities throughout the country; prices may be higher or lower than these listed in this chapter. The best way to know exactly what the costs might be in your own area is to contact the local funeral home or homes and ask for the appropriate information. In past years this data was sometimes difficult to obtain, but now with a new federal law which took affect in 1984, funeral homes must give this information over the phone.

Congregations can also do a great deal for their members by looking at several of the funeral homes in the area and making public the various prices that are current. The church could then distribute such a brochure to its members. We have put such a piece together at Prince of Peace and would be happy to share a copy with anyone who requests it. Please write for the "Preparing for Death" brochure, Prince of Peace Publishing, 13801 Fairview Drive, Burnsville, Minnesota 55337. We will charge a nominal fee for printing and mailing.

EXTRA FUNERAL EXPENSES

*C*askets are unquestionably the major cost item in a funeral. However, there are many other costs which may be incurred. Some of these may be considered to be essentials by some buyers, and others will seem unnecessary. Again, it is recommended that buyers be clear on what is covered in the basic funeral price and what is considered to be extra. It is best to have these prices in writing, so that the consumer can purchase only those goods and services which are truly desired. This chapter will highlight some of those extras which are offered. The *Consumers Union Report* is the source of a good deal of this information.

1. Embalming

Second only in importance to the casket, from the funeral director's frame of reference, is the issue of embalming. To clarify, embalming is not usually considered to be a separate or deductible item in funerals; most funeral directors include this in the essentials. In fact, embalming is often performed routinely, even without the permission of the family. Those who have looked closely at the funeral industry have found that it sometimes is included in the total cost even if it is not done.

However, sometimes buyers can't win no matter what happens. If a family requests that embalming not be done, some funeral homes will add an additional charge for refrigeration, and this can cost the family almost as much as the embalming.

Embalming is absolutely necessary in the eyes of many funeral directors, for it forms the basis for the sale of other profitable merchandise. It leads to the marketing of cosmetics, burial clothes, and shoes, and ornately lined and cushioned caskets. It also has the effect of keeping the customer dealing with the same funeral home. Once the body has been embalmed it is very difficult for a family to take the remains somewhere else.

Embalming and the art of restoration have long been essential parts of the conventional American funeral. Since the turn of the century, most Americans have been selecting open caskets for their loved ones. Many believe that this custom is a part of the "traditional" religious ceremony. But in reality, this experience has no roots in either Christian or Jewish religions. In fact, it is even contrary to Orthodox Jewish law. Nor is embalming common outside of the United States and Canada.

Legal requirements concerning embalming vary greatly from state to state. Generally, however, it is not necessary according to state law to embalm, unless the body is transported from one state to another, or unless death results from a communicable disease. Embalming must also be done if the final disposition of the body does not occur within 72 hours. In addition, in some states a body must be embalmed if it is to be transported within the state and will not arrive at the city or town in which burial will occur within 18 hours from the time of death. It is best to check the state statutes.

Sometimes funeral directors will state or at least imply that embalming is required by law. That is not the case except in those situations listed above. Embalming is also encouraged by the suggestion that it will bring about long-term preservation of the body. There is no evidence that this is the case. Most of the time embalming only preserves the body through the time of the funeral. In any case, the body which dies is supposed to return to the earth, "Dust to dust, ashes to ashes, earth to earth," and nothing can or should ultimately prevent this.

Other Extras

Sometimes an extra might be rather difficult to describe. It certainly varies from one funeral home to another. But basically each funeral home has a rather standard group of goods and services which are available which are listed as making up the "complete" funeral. Thus, when referring to extras, we are talking about those things which are not a part of that standard group, those which would be billed as over and above the set cost.

Some of these would include:

Flowers	Musicians
Burial clothing	Prayer cards
Additional vehicles	Memorial books and cards
Clergy honorarium	Sympathy cards
Newspaper death notices	Acknowledgment cards
Hired pallbearers	Gratuities
Transcripts and death certificates	Sales tax
	Other transportation

Besides these, some funeral homes also sell such items as crucifixes, Bibles, memorial flag cases, and the list could go on indefinitely.

Many of the extra goods and services in a funeral are listed on the bill as "cash advances" or "accommodations". This means that the funeral home has advanced the funds on behalf of the buyer for certain items, and these must be repaid by the customer.

Funeral directors often claim that there is little profit in these extras. This may be true in comparison with the large profits made on the casket or other major services such as embalming. But the selection of a number of these extras can prove to be a considerable source of income for the funeral home. Because funeral directors frequently obtain discounts from sellers of cash advance items, such extras can yield substantial profits.

The remainder of this chapter will be devoted to a closer look at some of the most common extras.

3. Flowers

The average American funeral typically includes about 20 floral displays, without counting those from the immediate family. Flowers are important at funerals; they can be very comforting for the bereaved and also provide an opportunity for friends and loved ones to give loving tributes to the deceased.

However, large numbers of floral displays are not necessary, nor perhaps very helpful at the time of a funeral. This remains of course a family decision, but sometimes we have tended to gauge the popularity or status of a person by the number of floral arrangements present at the funeral. It is not hard to understand why this kind of measure is totally inappropriate, but there is the temptation to do this nevertheless. We must state emphatically that flowers neither enhance nor detract from a person's worth or value.

There are many families today who are actively discouraging the giving of flowers at the time of a funeral. There is a more recent development, but it seems to be happening more frequently. Families have determined that flowers very seldom last more than a few days and then are thrown away. Gifts which can continue to give for a longer period of time are often recommended instead. Memorial funds are established, and friends are then encouraged to give to this fund instead of purchasing flowers.

If a family wishes to indicate such a preference, that gifts be given to a memorial fund instead of going for flowers, this can be done in the printed obituary in the paper. It can read "memorials preferred in lieu of flowers" or "no flowers". As we might expect, there has been substantial pressure by the floral industry on newspapers not to print such announcements. Because of the clout of the industry and its influential advertising budget, there are some newspapers which will not print the words "in lieu of flowers". That sounds rather amazing, but it is true. However, in most cases if a family wishes to limit the amount of flowers and direct the gifts toward a memorial fund, there is a way to do this.

In checking with florists in our community, we find that average prices in 1985 are as follows:

Casket Spray . . . . $75–$100
Easel spray (roses and carnations) $55– $80
Stands $2– $5
Pot spray (glads, spider mums) $25– $55
Wreaths (carnations) $35– $50
Cross on easel $45– $60
Lid / grandparent
   (small cross of heart, mums and roses $20– $26
Small pillow (roses) $12– $20
Ribbons . . . . No charge to $3
Delivery within the city $3.50– $4.50

Other suggestions for flowers include ferns, plants, and dish gardens, which can be sent to the home for a remembrance. The most popular flowers are glads, mums, and carnations. Roses are for the family or special reasons.

Many churches today are limiting the amount of floral displays which can be placed in front of the sanctuary at the time of a funeral. Our congregation, for instance, recommends that only the flowers given by the immediate family may be placed in the sanctuary. If the family wishes, other flowers may be displayed in some other places in the church. This should be discussed with the pastor.

4. Obituary

An obituary is a biographical sketch of the deceased. By printing this in the local newspaper, those beyond the immediate family and friends can be informed about the death and the subsequent plans for a service and/or visitation. Obituaries generally state the name, age, city, survivors, and perhaps some general history of the life which has been lived.

Any person can contact the newspaper with this information; it need not be the funeral director. There is usually no cost for most local or small town papers. this is a part of their service to that community.

However, the cost for the printing of an obituary in a major metropolitan newspaper can be considerable. By way of example, the major newspaper in the area where I serve charges $3.65 per line one weekdays and $4.70 per line on Sundays.

Most often this information is called in by the funeral director, and the cost is often less in such circumstances. In other words, in some places it is cheaper for the funeral director to call in such a notice than for any of us. I suppose this is because the newspaper will have to spend time in verification if it is a private party, while a funeral director is a known quantity to the paper. There may be other reasons also.

One word of caution is in order concerning obituaries which are published in the paper. Unfortunately, some in our society use the obituaries to prey on people who are going through pain and grief. The time when the family will be gone from their home at a visitation or a service is often listed clearly in the obituary. This is almost an open invitation for some to try and break into the home. Thus, it is well to have someone present in the home while the family is away at a publicly announced visitation or reviewal, with all of the lights on, in order to protect the property from those who seek to steal.

In addition, obituary notices in the paper sometimes become a mailing or calling list for those who are trying to sell goods or services. I would strongly suggest that families resist any attempt to make contact with them based on information gained from an obituary. It is just not an appropriate use of that information.

5. Burial Clothing

Clothing is another extra which often sells well in the funeral home. Many funeral buyers feel that an entirely new outfit is required for burial even though the clothing of the deceased may be perfectly suitable, and the lower part of the casket is closed. Most moderate-to-large sized funeral homes display garments for the dead: shoes, stockings, underwear or lingeries, shirts, suits, tuxedos, dresses, negligees, and pajamas. For those who have never encountered such a thing, I am not kidding. This is for real. And the cost of such special burial clothing can be significant, for the majority of it is made of silk or satin.

There are generally more clothes available for women than for men. One clothing firm reports manufacturing just five basic styles for men and more than 250 for women, exclusive of custom orders. About 80 standard dress sizes are offered in a variety of colors.

I believe personally that purchases of clothing at the funeral home are generally unnecessary. There is hardly a person in our society who does not have an appropriate outfit of clothing in the closet which could be used for burial. This should not be a difficult decision for most persons; however, in Chapter 15 there is documented a rather bizarre story which gives another perspective on the selection of burial clothing.

6. Transportation

Transportation can be one of the costliest extras. this can be true even if the funeral takes place in the same community where the death occurred, if the cemetery is beyond a certain distance. But transportation is especially costly when out-of-town travel is necessary. Extras such as the ambulance, or "first-call car" which picks up the body and takes it to the funeral home, the hearse, flower cars, limousines for survivors and other mourners, all raise the overall cost of funerals. Funeral vehicles are very expensive.

The majority of funeral homes will own some vehicles. Others will lease or rent instead. But owned, leased, or rented vehicles will often show up as a separate item in the funeral buyer's bill. Generally only the hearse and one limousine are included in the price of the "complete" funeral. If it is necessary to transport a body from one community to another, it can substantially increase the cost of the funeral.

Consumers Union estimates that every year some 200,000 bodies are transported by air, rail or hearse to out-of-town locations in the United States. Today the majority of bodies are shipped by air, and rates for this shipping are anywhere from 175% to 250% more than the rates for other air freight.

Very often the extra expense incurred in the transportation of bodies is something people do not consider, especially when wishing to be buried in another city, state or country. This can often impose a real financial hardship on the survivors.

If survivors find themselves in a situation where it is necessary to arrange for transportation of the remains over a considerable distance, one cardinal rule should be followed. If a relative or friend dies in a distant locality, but is buried in another place, *never* contact the funeral home in the place where the death occurs. Always call the funeral home in the community wehre the funeral is to take place. Otherwise you will pay for the equivalent of two funerals.

7. Clergy

Very often the funeral home will charge the family for an honorarium to be paid to the officiating clergy. Many pastors find this practice distressing and some have managed to convince the funeral director that this is not appropriate. However, other pastors are rather relieved that the funeral director will expedite this matter, so the pastor will not have to deal with the family regarding this issue.

I realize that every clergyperson has his or her own position on this rather touchy issue. I also understand fully how underpaid most clergy tend to be, and income from funerals is sometimes a vital part of their compensation. So at the risk of offending just about everyone, let me state our policy.

We do not accept honorariums from the funerals of church members. We make this clear in the funeral brochure that we give to each person. If people insist on giving such a gift, we do not argue with them, we just donate it to the memorial fund which has been established. However, we do accept honorariums for those funerals we lead of non-members, but we do not suggest any specific fee. These policies have seemed to work well for us.

In summary, in all areas of funeral planning and purchasing, buyers must be aggressive in seeking information about prices. Some extras will be unavoidable in a conventional funeral, and people should be free to purchase what is truly desired. It is also important to note that many funeral directors are very sensitive to the financial state of the family and will attempt to discourage some purchases. But we should be aware that many costs may be unnecessary, and the buyer should understand completely what is offered and what is essential.

CEMETERIES

*I*t is most surprising to find how few people have actually chosen the place for burial. However, this is the case, and in my own experience it appears as if most families must make this decision after the death of a loved one. It is really not fair. There is often only an hour or two in which to decide, but that is the way it is usually done. In more rural areas, this may not be an issue, but in urban communities this can be a very difficult choice.

During the previous two centuries, cemeteries were located for the most part in the middle of towns or churchyards, where burial was usually restricted to the members of the congregation or community. Because there were not sufficient funds set aside for the upkeep of such cemeteries, many of them fell into disuse.

At the same time, governmental bodies began to recognize that some new directions were necessary in providing space for burials. Thus, many new cemeteries were established on the outskirts of urban areas and in suburban communities. Municipalities began to assume more responsibility for these burial grounds, and laws and regulations were put into place to govern them. In many states, burial grounds were then supported by public funds, even though many of them remained private.

Historically, both the church and municipal cemeteries charged modest burial fees, but in neither case was burying the dead considered to be a profit-making enterprise. It was only in this century that developers began to buy land with the purpose of making profits on the sale of grave plots. Because land costs were often low and property bought for burial purposes was tax-exempt, the cemetery proved to be quite popular as an investment. Each acre of land could be divided into numerous plots, and because of the cemetery's nonprofit status, owners did not have to pay income taxes on the proceeds from the sale of grave plots.

At present it is estimated by the American Cemetery Association that nearly 25% of the cemeteries in the United States are publicly owned, operated by cities, counties, states and local tax districts. About 17% are church affiliated. A small fraction, about 2%, are owned by fraternal organizations and cooperatives. An additional 20% are operated by other types of nonprofit associations. The largest number, however, 36%, are privately or corporately owned and managed, and these cemeteries are operated for profit.

Cemetery costs usually cover four areas:

1. The plot of ground for the casket.
2. The burial enclosure, the vault or liner. These are not required by state law, but *are* required by most cemeteries.
3. Opening or closing the grave or entombment.
4. The memorial (marker, monument, or plaque).

In addition, many cemeteries also charge for installing or setting a monument or marker at the grave site. Some cemeteries also charge for the perpetual cost of the grave site. Others consider perpetual care to be a part of the price of a lot, and a certain percentage of the price is set aside in a trust fund for this purpose. Some states requrie such funding by law.

Cemetery Lots

There are many factors which go into the selection of a cemetery plot. It is important to decide how many plots will be needed right from the beginning, understanding clearly which family members will be buried in this location. Often couples will purchase two plots for themselves, leaving the decision about burial plots for their children to the next generation. These children will most likely have their own families and will want to decide this for themselves, especially if there is a strong likelihood that the children will reside in locales different from their parents'.

Such a decision is also influenced by family history and tradition. It has much to do with the sense of continuity with the past, or lack of it. Is it important to be buried where one's parents and other relatives have been buried? Or is it more important to make this decision based on other considerations: location, church affiliation, present family arrangements?

If this decision is made ahead of time, and it is far better to do so, it is important that it be considered carefully. A buyer should always go and visit the cemetery, inspect the grounds, facilities and upkeep. The plot should be examined to see if this is exactly what is desired. All of the various charges for such a plot should be investigated, so there are no surprises for one's family. Planning ahead is always best.

If a plot is to be purchased on a time-payment plan, as most of them are, a buyer should be clear about the interest charged by the cemetery. Some cemeteries do not charge interest at all, and among those which do, there is a great diversity in charges. If the cemetery charges a high rate of interest, a buyer should be able to save money by taking out a lower-interest loan from a bank or credit union.

Some cemeteries include in the price of the plot or crypt the cost of perpetual care. Typically 10% or more of the price is set aside for this purpose. Municipal and other nonprofit cemeteries may allocate a larger percentage. Others often charge a separate fee. This money goes into what was called an endowment care fund, which is placed in trust. Its earnings then are used to maintain the grounds or mausoleums in perpetuity.

Some states require such funding by law. A prospective buyer should discover whether the funds in the cemetery under consideration are sufficient to maintain the plot or crypt. In many cases, a state agency is responsible for the proper administration of the trust fund, and a buyer can check with the appropriate agency about the provisions for endowment care of the cemetery. If perpetual care is optional, a buyer should inspect the grave sites with and without the special care to determine whether they are worth a premium.

Costs vary widely for the purchase of cemetery plots. In our larger urban area, plots range from around $200 all the way up to $1,500. The average in 1987 is in the range of $500. Some cemeteries are now offering a plan by which two caskets can be placed in the same plot, one on top of the other. This would lessen the amount of cost for the plot.

In more rural areas, the cost for cemetery plots is considerably less. Just outside of our city, the cost of these plots is from $125 to $150. Wherever land prices are lower in cost, the cemetery would tend to have lower costs for grave plots. These costs can be easily checked by a phone call.

2. Vaults and Liners

These grave enclosures are very seldom, if ever, included in the listed funeral price, but can add a considerable amount to the total cost of the funeral. There is no state law requiring vaults or grave liners, but most cemeteries do require them. It is highly questionable whether a vault has any real value. Any claims of protection of the body are challenged vociferously by many critics, who wonder whether there is any way at all to truly protect the body. More importantly, many ask whether this should even be a goal. Is it essential to try and protect the body, or should the body be allowed to return to the earth? Each family needs to make this decision based on solid information, and then on what seems best to them.

There are two basic kinds of grave enclosures. The first is a prefabricated two-part coffin enclosure of steel and concrete, usually sold by the funeral director. The reasons given for such a vault usually include, as was previously mentioned, protection of the body and prevention of the ground from settling. In the recent past, cemeteries merely kept a big pile of dirt in the vicinity, and when a grave plot settled, they would fill in the empty space with dirt. However, there is tremendous profit in the selling of vaults, so it has become a common part of the funeral industry.

There is also a grave liner, a lower cost container with a concrete bottom, two concrete end pieces and two concrete side pieces. About three out of four caskets are placed in some type of enclosure at the time of burial, about four of every five of these being sold by the funeral director.

The costs of the liners or vaults vary greatly. They generally are less expensive when purchased from a cemetery than from a funeral director. Grave enclosures begin at about $300 and rise to more than $1700. At a nearby funeral home the cost of a concrete liner begins at $400 and rises to $1675.

The Federal Trade Commission says that the wholesale to retail markup on vaults is seldom less than 100%, and sometimes as high as 500% to 600%. Thus, it is not surprising that the funeral director prefers that the customer buy an internment receptacle from him rather than from a cemetery, and thus purchase a more expensive one. To illustrate the competition that is present, there are some cemeteries in our community which try to compete with the funeral home in the sale of vaults by charging extra to bury a vault purchased at a funeral home.

The Consumers Union gives a more complete description of some of the options which are available. One Midwest burial firm, which sells almost exclusively to funeral directors, offers reinforced concrete vaults in nine price brackets. The top six come with a personalized nameplate and in a variety of colors. These include as many as 11 "enhancing finishes to complement any casket selection". The least expensive concrete vaults are made of natural unpainted concrete. Metal vaults sold by the firm include steel, stainless steel, and copper models, available in eight different price brackets.

For many years the Veterans Administration National Cemetery System did not provide vaults or grave liners in its cemeteries. But in 1975 a test program using government supplied grave liners was begun in ten of the active cemeteries to see if maintenance problems of sunken graves and tipped headstones could be solved. Test results were so favorable that now most of the national cemeteries use grave liners, and they have been specified for new national cemeteries now nearing completion.

A national cemetery is open to any person who has served in the Armed Forces and was honorably discharged, or any member of the Reserves who dies under honorable conditions while serving on active duty. Also the spouse, widow, or widower, is eligible for burial, as well as minor children under the age of 21. A spouse of a deceased veteran who remarries is not eligible for burial. However, if the second marriage of the spouse is terminated by death or divorce, then this person is again eligible for burial in a national cemetery. There is no charge for a cemetery plot at a national cemetery, for the opening and closing of the grave, or for the headstone.

3. Opening and Closing the Grave

The cost to a cemetery for opening and closing a grave takes about 30 minutes and is not very much, but the cost to the consumer can be high. Some cemeteries' charges will vary depending on what is used, a vault or concrete liner, because the cost of this enclosure is less. They will charge less to place a vault into the ground, because the profits are greater on the original sale. In almost all cemeteries, the opening and closing fee will be higher when the internment or entombment takes place late in the afternoon, on Sundays or on holidays. National cemeteries are not open on either Saturday or Sunday.

In my own community, the costs for opening and closing a grave are between $250 and $400 in 1985. In the more rural areas, the cost is much less, about $100 to $135. The substantial difference has little to do with the cost of the service, but rather the increased overhead and profit needs of the urban cemeteries.

4. Memorials, Markers, Monuments and Plaques

Almost all cemeteries have strict regulations and restrictions governning the placement and size of monuments and markers. Many cemeteries sell a standard size to be used for both single and double markers. Many also have rules about the kinds of material that may be used in memorials, usually requiring granite, bronze and marble. Other materials such as cement, artificial stone and iron are rarely prescribed. Cemeteries can even regulate, to some extent, the wording or inscriptions on the memorials.

More and more of the new memorial park cemeteries are requiring markers set flush with the ground, making the overall maintenance of the grounds far easier. An increasing number of cemeteries today are selling their own memorials, increasing their profits. In most urban areas there are more flat markers to be found; in rural areas there are more monuments.

In my own community, the costs for markers range from about $200 to more than $1,150. The material, size, craftsmanship and design of a marker or monument can affect the price as well as the number of engraved letters in the inscription. The average size for markers is about two feet long and one foot wide. They vary in thickness from six to ten inches. Contemporary monuments are normally two and one-half feet high, three and one-half feet in width and about eight inches thick.

Most flat markers are made of granite or bronze, with granite markers by far the most common.

Most cemeteries have specific requirements concerning decorations, such as flowers, plants, urns, vases, as well as ground charges for plot improvement. A number of cemeteries require that their own vases or urns be used at grave sites, and artificial flowers and wreaths are not permitted. In addition, fresh flowers are usually removed after a certain time has elapsed.

In summary, the costs at the cemetery can be considerable. They are not usually listed in the costs of a funeral by the funeral director, so it is necessary for the buyer to be very clear on what these charges will be. Again, it is highly recommended that this decision be made far in advance of the actual need, so that the family doesn't have to struggle with it at the time of death.

ALTERNATIVES TO THE CONVENTIONAL FUNERAL

*F*or most of our history, there was no question but that at the time of death there would quickly follow a burial in the ground. The body was most often placed into a simple wood coffin and lowered into the earth. "Dust to dust, ashes to ashes, earth to earth," were the words that accompanied such an act. Recently though some things have begun to change and some new alternatives to earth burials have become available.

Much of the change has been caused by the rapidly accelerating costs of a burial. Part of this is due to the declining cemetery space available. It has become increasingly difficult for our urban areas to set aside sufficient land for earth burials. And when there are fewer choices for burial, very often the cost will rise. Thus, we have seen in recent years a move toward considering some other alternatives.

1. Cremation

The most common of these alternatives is that of cremation, which has become far more popular in the latter part of the 20th century. At the beginning of the 1980s, approximately 11% of all the funerals in the United States utilized cremation. In states such as California and Florida, the percentage is closer to 50%, and in other countries around the world, the percentage is often even higher. For instance, about 59% of those who died in Great Britain were cremated, and in the Scandinavian countries the number is even greater.

What is cremation? Cremation is very simply reducing the human body through a hot flame to ashes and bone fragments. In essence, it does in just a few moments what would happen over a much longer period of time. The end results are the same, the body returns to the earth, but the time frame is quite different.

The religious community has not wholeheartedly supported cremation in the past. There is no biblical injunction against this practice, but there was rather widespread resistance and even opposition to its use. Gradually in recent years, however, most Western religions have lessened their opposition, and support has greatly increased.

Until 1963, the Roman Catholic church was strongly opposed to cremation. Burial was affirmed as the proper and traditional method of final disposition. The argument given was that this was following the example of Jesus' burial. Cremation was even forbidden by a decree in 1886 as being irreligious, anti-clerical and hostile to the belief in the immortality of the soul and the resurrection of the body. The church regarded proponents of cremation as "enemies of the Christian faith". In addition, strong penalties were imposed to anyone who utilized cremation, such as a refusal of a Christian burial and in some cases, excommunication. Yet cremation was never opposed by the church on theological grounds; it was not considered to be contrary to dogma or divine law.

The Roman Catholic position was changed in 1963, and today members incur no penalties if they choose cremation under certain conditions. Catholics who wish to be cremated must obtain permission from the chancery office of their diocese, which will decide whether the reasons for the request are acceptable to the church. The church still urges its members to religiously maintain the custom of burial and asks bishops to instruct Catholics not to choose cremation except for serious reasons. Many Catholics, however, are still unaware that the church now allows cremations.

There are also some other religious bodies which still maintain strong opposition to cremation. Mohammedanism, Orthodox

Orthodox and Conservative Judaism are examples. The Lutheran Church Missouri Synod has sometimes in the past opposed cremation, although this has changed dramatically. Some conservative and fundamentalistic Protestant denominations have also looked with disfavor. Mormons may choose cremation, but it is discouraged by the church. The Eastern Orthodox churches also do not favor it.

I believe that most Christians today accept the fact that cremation is not against the teachings of the Bible, nor somehow unchristian. From a Christian perspective it is as fully acceptable as an earth burial. Some people may find it to be distasteful for one reason or another, but there is no validity in giving this personal dislike any theological justification. Cremation does not interfere with the resurrection of the body, as some might fear, because in the resurrection we will receive a brand new body. The results of each burial and cremation are the same; the body returns to the ground, and there is no way to prevent this.

Most larger cities have crematories, and a number of them are associated with cemeteries. By way of example, in Minnesota there is an organization called the Cremation Society of Minnesota, which is affiliated with a specific funeral home. This society has a basic fee of $445 for members, and $495 for nonmembers. To become a member of this society requires a one-time membership fee of $15.

Funeral homes in most cases will also arrange for a cremation. The cost in 1987 was about $500 to $800 for the least expensive cremation and minimal service. A casket is not needed if a cremation takes place, which of course limits the overall cost substantially. In the past, some funeral directors have insisted that a casket was needed even for a cremation, but the strong response of the regulatory agencies has almost eliminated that claim.

There are several options for disposing for the cremated remains:

1. Purchase an urn and place in a colubarium.
2. Have the remains buried in a cemetery. There are smaller plots which may be purchased for this purpose.
3. In some states, the remains can be buried on private property.

4. In most states, the option is available to scatter the remains on land or at sea or to hire someone else to do this.

The laws concerning cremation may vary from state to state, as suggested above, but in almost every state people cannot legally determine their final method of disposition. A deceased person's final instructions to be cremated, whether written or given verbally while alive, are not legally binding after death. Thus the manner of disposition is decided by the next of kin, executor, or legal custodian. Of course, many survivors are willing to carry out the loved one's wishes; but some assume that in order for a cremation to be performed legally, specific instructions must have been provided by the deceased. This is not the case.

All states require a permit for burial or a transit for burial. However, only a few require a special permit for cremation and disposition of the remains.

As might be expected, many cemetery operators are often opposed to the scattering of cremated remains, since their profits come primarily from the sale of urns and columbarium niches or grave plots.

People who choose cremation and wish to keep the overall cost as low as possible have several options. The *Consumer's Union* suggests the following:

1. If there is a memorial society in the community, the most inexpensive cremation is probably available through membership in the society. Members of most memorial societies can arrange for formal funeral services first, if desired, followed by cremation. Non-members usually may also obtain the name of cremation firms from these societies.

2. Commercial firms which specialize in simple direct cremation services are another alternative.

3. If cremation is arranged through a regular funeral home, and if funeral services are desired, the choice of a simple container can help to minimize costs. In some funeral homes, a casket can be rented for the visitation and the service, if cremation is then to take place. In my own experience, the cost of renting a casket is about one-half the price of purchasing one. Survivors should

make inquiries about the cremator's requirements concerning containers and caskets.

4. The purchase of an urn is not necessary for burial. Cremated remains can be buried in a simple canister or special container in which they are placed after removal from the cremation chamber. Survivors can also provide their own urns, although if an urn is placed in a columbarium in a niche with a glass facing, the management may reserve the right to approve any special or unusual container.

5. Some crematories bury urns in unmarked areas on their grounds at low cost. Other crematories provide inexpensive permanent storage for urns in large vaults.

In summary, cremations are becoming more common. There is no Christian or biblical reason why a cremation could not be considered. This decision should be made by the family based on the wishes of the deceased, on the tradition and beliefs of the family, and on a consideration of the costs involved. Again, it is far better to make such a decision in advance, rather than leaving it to the survivors after a death has occurred.

2. Memorial Societies

A new and growing phenomenon in recent years has been the emergence of memorial societies. These arose largely out of reaction to what was perceived as the high cost of traditional funerals. They established a goal to provide disposition of the body at a much lower cost. These societies are by and large non-profit, democratic and cooperative. They usually operate on small budgets and are staffed primarily by volunteers. They look at themselves as advocates for the consumer, organized to protest the high cost of dying and to offer alternatives.

Memorial societies are open to all and are joined with a one-time fee, usually no more than $20. The societies center their emphasis on the goals of simplicity, dignity and economy and focus on the right of each individual to make the final decision about the disposition of his or her own body. All of the societies provide literature concerning the various alternatives for disposition, including cremation and bequeathal of the body or body organs to medical science. Memorial societies are primarily educational in nature, encouraging the open discussion of funeral arrangements in advance of the time when there is a real need.

There are basically three types of memorial societies.

a. Contract Society

This kind of society has a formal arrangement with some local funeral directors to provide society members with prear-ranged funeral services at less than regular costs. In other words, the society serves as a kind of broker helping the consumer to find a lower cost funeral. Contract funeral directors will usually be guaranteed sufficient volume to compensate for their setting of lower prices for society members.

When a person enrolls in a memorial society, he or she is then given a number of educational resources to help the decision-making process. These include the types of services available, the names of the contract funeral directors and the information about body and organ donation programs. A new member selects that plan which seems to be best and fills out the necessary forms. Usually three or four copies of each form are required: one for the memorial society's files, one to be sent to the funeral director, and one for the clergyperson, if desired.

These forms should be kept with one's important papers, but not in the safety deposit box. Most memorial socities issue identifi-cation cards for members to carry with them, including the name and address of the contract funeral director.

By way of example, the Minnesota Memorial Society offered four options in 1985. The membership fee was $15. These in-cluded:

1) Simple Cremation / $400

Cremation is provided and the remains are placed in a suit-able container as soon as is practical after a death. This includes the removal of the body from the place of death, all transportation charges within a 20-mile radius of the funeral home, obtaining death certificates, cremation permit, and crematory charges. There is no embalming or reviewal, but a funeral chapel is avail-able for a memorial service. This also can be held in a church.

There is no arrangement for the disposition of the ashes, nor assistance in collecting death benefits from Social Security, veteran's benefits, etc.

2) Simple Burial / $525

This provides an immediate burial in a casket of very modest means, according to the member's wishes. There is the removal of the body from the place of death, together with all transportation charges within a 20-mile radius of the funeral home. It also includes the obtaining of the death certificate and burial permit. There is no embalming or reviewal, but a funeral chapel is available for memorial services. This includes assistance in collecting death benefits from Social Security and veteran's benefits, but does not allow for any cemetery expenses.

3) Cremation with Funeral Service / $625

This option includes a worship service at a church or a funeral chapel with the body present in a closed casket. The cremation will then follow this service. This includes the removal of the body from the place of death, all transportation charges within a 20-mile radius of the funeral home, obtaining of the death certificate and cremation permit, as well as crematory charges. There is no embalming or reviewal. This includes assistance in the arrangements for the ashes and in collecting death benefits.

4) Burial with Funeral Service / $575

This includes a service to be held either at a church or a funeral chapel with the body present in a closed casket, followed by a burial. Removal of the body from the place of death, all transportation charges within a 20-mile radius of the funeral home, and obtaining of the death certificate and burial permit are included. This also provides assistance in collecting death benefits. These charges do not include cemetery expenses, obituary notices, unusual travel or delay, embalming, grave liner, grave markers, or grave opening or closing. Transportation charges beyond 20 miles are currently 65 cents a mile.

b. Cooperating Society

A second kind of memorial society is called a cooperating society. This is a society without a formal contract with a funeral director, but where an understanding or verbal agreement exists with at least one funeral home. In this way it saves the survivors the task of searching for moderate cost facilities when they are under severe time pressure.

c. Advisory Society

The third kind of memorial society only occurs rarely, but it may be present when a society has not been able to find a contract or cooperating funeral home. The society would then become mostly a clearing house for information and education. Frequently, funeral directors who cooperate with memorial societies are subject to pressure and ostracism from the rest of the industry and, on occasion, even face disciplinary measures from the state board of funeral directors.

In general, resistance by funeral directors to memorial societies has diminished somewhat, but opposition is still the rule, particularly in the South and Southwest. A funeral director who chooses to become involved with memorial societies or with cremation societies sometimes is not very popular with his or her peers. As I heard one such funeral director quoted, "If I wanted to find friends, I would have joined the YMCA." In other words, there is not much support for maverick funeral directors, and they often must go it alone.

More information about the nearest memorial society can be found by writing to the Continental Association of Funeral and Memorial Societies, 1828 L Street N.W., Washington, DC 20036, and the phone number is 202-293-4821. In Canada one may contact the Memorial Society Association of Canada, 5326 Ada Boulevard, Edmonton, Alberta T5W 4N7.

3. Reviewal and Cremation

Some funeral homes are offering another alternative. There is also the possibility of a reviewal, followed by a cremation, which can take place either before the service or after. Some of these funeral homes, as mentioned above, will provide a rental casket for this purpose; it can be used during the reviewal and/or the service, and then a cremation can take place. The cost of the rental of the casket for the two or three days is not inexpensive; it can be one-half of the cost of the casket or more. However, this still provides a substantial savings in the overall cost of the funeral.

4. Low-Cost Options

Most funeral homes have a low-cost option which is available. This alternative is not usually mentioned; it will only be revealed if asked for specifically. Usually, this low-cost option includes the four basic services which need to be provided:

1. Pick up the body from the place of death.
2. Bring the body to the church where appropriate.
3. Transport the body to the cemetery.
4. Take care of the death certificate.

This does not include the cost of the casket or any burial costs. In 1987, funeral homes in our community would provide these basic services for just under $800.

5. Pre-Need Plans

A growing number of people are planning ahead for their own funeral. This is all to the good. This looking to the future often involves some kind of financial planning in addition to the specifics of the funeral. For instance, some people will set aside money in a savings account, trust fund, or credit union account to cover the funeral expenses. Others will plan to have their life insurance provide such support, or they will even purchase a separate policy.

In addition, some will also prepay or prefinance a funeral or burial through what is called a "pre-need" plan. Here a buyer will select the goods and services that are desired and sign a contract to pay for such items in advance of the need. this is usually set up on an installment basis. Pre-need plans may be bought either through a funeral home or a cemetery, or through a pre-need sales firm, many of whom sell door-to-door. There is often a less-than-honorable record from these sales firms.

In many states, all money paid to a pre-need plan must be deposited in a savings account or trust fund. The interest can then be used to offset the effects of inflation. If a pre-need account is established, one must make sure that the following questions are answered in writing:

1. What will happen if the funeral home is not in existence when the death occurs?
2. If you would change your mind and wish to make other arrangements, can this be done? You may move to a new location, or other circumstances may change your intentions.
3. What happens if the person dies before all of the installments are paid?
4. Can the money you pay be refunded?

There are two alternatives which might be considered instead of purchasing a pre-need plan.

1. Establish an interest-bearing account dedicated to funeral costs.

2. Establish a Totten Trust. This may be done in a credit union, bank or other savings institution. Such a trust is simply a savings account to which you add the name of the beneficiary. It can be in trust for a funeral director or a friend or relative who is entrusted to use the funds as you direct. The advantage of this arrangement is that the funds stay in your control and can be withdrawn in case of an emergency, or if you should move to another location.

To summarize, I would strongly discourage having a pre-need sales firm come into your home to make a presentation. There is often a good deal of high pressure that accompanies such a sales attempt. Often when you call a funeral home or cemetery to ask about costs, someone will try to arrange a visit in your home to explain all of the specifics. They claim that it is too complicated an explanation to make over the phone.

Do not be misled. This is often a very concentrated attempt to convince you to buy some goods and services, usually at a high cost. Obviously, a portion of these costs will go to pay the sales commission. If you have difficulty, as I do, in saying no to the persistent salesperson, then it is better to resist such a visit before it happens. There are better ways to prepare for funeral plans.

THE FUNERAL SERVICE

*W*orship is at the center of our life together as the Christian community. All persons involved in congregational leadership should give as much attention and care to worship as possible. The funeral service is, above all else, a time of worship and should be given the same importance and value as all other worship. It is best held in the church sanctuary, where the symbols, the music, the altar and the entire setting can be a part of the theme of Christian hope. This worship should focus primarily on God and his love for us, on the promise of the resurrection we have in Jesus Christ, and on the comfort of the Holy Spirit and the people of God. If we can communicate the Gospel in all of its fullness at the time of a funeral worship, we have indeed been an effective witness.

Some churches try to distinguish between funerals for members and non-members. There are many ways by which a first-class and second-class impression may be given. I believe that at the time of a funeral all of these distinctions are irrelevant and counterproductive. Our role as the community of faith is to provide ministry, healing and love to anyone who is in need. Congregations which turn away any family at the time of death are taking a stance which is contrary to the spirit of the Gospel and the love of Christ.

At the time of a funeral, we should be the most inclusive community in the world. Our task is to minister to the living and to bring comfort to the grieving, not to try to make some human judgments about the deceased. That belongs to God. If we somehow avoid or ignore an opportunity to care for a hurting family, if our own needs come before the needs of bereaved people, then we have lost an important dimension of the Gospel.

This emphasis is also true when we discuss the kind of death that has taken place. Some congregations refuse to allow the funeral of one who has committed suicide, or who has died in what is judged to be a less-than-honorable way. Again, this is a violation of our call to be ministers of Jesus Christ, who did not turn people away. We certainly do not want to give any false impression to people about "cheap grace", but we do want to be there for any persons who have suffered the painful and heartwrenching loss of a loved one. The time to take a stand about who may or may not be a part of the kingdom of God is not at a funeral. We are open to anyone who asks us to provide a worship service for one who has died.

William Poovey, in his book *Planning a Christian Funeral*, suggests five reasons why the Christian funeral is so important.

1. Funerals satisfy the need of people to do something for the person who has died. It helps us relieve our sense of helplessness. There is something to do, something to plan, to move toward. While it would be easy to just not want to do anything, the funeral demands that the family work together in planning this important event.

2. Funerals help us accept the painful reality of death. Sometimes it is very easy to talk about death as just a transition, or as not being that traumatic to one who believes in eternal life. But death by its very nature is painful; it involves separation, heartache, loneliness and grief. The funeral focuses again on the finality and sting of death.

3. A funeral provides a time and a place for the release of emotions. We so often think that a Christian should be strong. If there is victory in death we should not be sad. However, the funeral

gives us opportunity, and maybe even encouragement, to mourn, and a time when we can express our honest emotions of grief and sorrow.

4. A funeral provides community and congregational support for the bereaved. Modern life today can often separate us from one another. We are often widely scattered. A funeral can bring us together to be in touch with each other. As Dr. Alvin Rogness writes, "Quite apart from anything you can say, your presence is the most eloquent language for the moment."

5. A funeral allows the church to proclaim its most significant belief, the resurrection. The ultimate comfort and triumph of the Gospel can be proclaimed in ringing terms. The funeral can give hope and comfort and the message of eternal life.

1. The Visitation

A time of visitation is often held before the funeral. It may be held at a funeral home, at the church, or in a private home. It may be with a casket present, or without. If there is a casket present, it may be opened or closed. A time of visitation is an important time of grieving, when people can weep with those who weep, when friends and loved ones can express compassion and concern to one another. It is often held the night before a funeral and may also be extended to the hour or two before the funeral service. It is an important time in the healing and grieving process, and we would strongly recommend such an event.

Often it is appropriate for a time of prayer or remembrance to take place at a visitation. Some traditions have a wake; others have more of an informal prayer service. If a family wishes some kind of prayer or sharing time at the visitation, this should be planned in close communication with the pastor.

2. The Order of Service

There are certain parts of the funeral worship service that we have found helpful. As was mentioned, above all it is important to center the service on the theme of Easter, to proclaim the resurrection of Jesus Christ. The music, the Scripture readings and the sermon should all be consistent with that theme. This is a service for the living, a time when those who grieve focus on their own needs and God's promises.

Music is a crucial part of a funeral service. One of the reasons why the church sanctuary is often the best place for such worship is because there is more opportunity for effective musical participation. There are found organs, hymnbooks and the tradition of singing.

I would strongly recommend that music be sung which is both theologically appropriate and also emotionally uplifting. There are many songs which very readily tear people apart, and it is best to avoid such sentimental fervor. Songs such as "Nearer My God to Thee" and "In the Garden" may be extremely hard on those who listen. The hymns and any solos should be chosen with much care and be committed to glorifying God as well as providing a sense of healing and help to those who are present.

We also encourage congregational singing at the time of a funeral service. This is a worship service, and singing together is most natural and positive. There are great hymns of the church which can lend so much comfort, strength and meaning at the time of death. Often, if we only have a solo or two, it can become more of a performance than a service of worship.

There are many hymns which can be recommended, and some of the decisions will depend on the specific hymnbook which is available where the service takes place. But in our own hymnbook, the following hymns are especially appropriate:

A Mighty Fortress Is Our God
All Glory, Laud and Honor
Amazing Grace, How Sweet the Sound
Beautiful Savior
Children of the Heavenly Father
Faith of Our Fathers, Living Still
For All the Saints, Who from Their Labors Rest
God of Our Fathers, Whose Almighty Hand
Hallelujah, Jesus Lives
How Great Thou Art
I Know That My Redeemer Lives
In Christ There Is No East or West

Jesus Shall Reign Wher'er the Sun
Joyful, Joyful We Adore Thee
Lead on, O King Eternal
Let All Things Now Living
Lift High the Cross, the Love of Christ Proclaim
Lord of All Hopefulness
Love Divine, All Loves Excelling
My God, How Wonderful Thou Art
My Hope Is Built on Nothing Less
Now Thank We All Our God
O Day Full of Grace That Now We See
O God, Our Help in Ages Past
O Master, Let Me Walk with Thee
Praise and Thanksgiving
Praise God from Whom All Blessings Flow
Praise to the Lord, the Almighty, the King of Creation
This Is My Father's World
We Praise You O God, Our Redeemer, Creator

3. Scripture Passages

One of the most important parts of the funeral service is the reading of Scripture passages. The promises of God are absolutely vital at a time like this, and the passages should be chosen with much care. Just as with music, there are some passages which are most appropriate, and others which would be better used at a different time. We want to concentrate on the resurrection, on the promises of God, on the comfort and hope we have in Jesus Christ. Some of the following passages might be used at a funeral worship:

Job 19:23-27a

"I know that my Redeemer lives, and at last he will stand upon the earth . . . then without my flesh I shall see God."

Psalm 23

"The Lord is my Shepherd . . . surely goodness and mercy shall follow me all the days of my life, and I shall dwell in the house of the Lord forever."

Psalm 27:1,4-5,13

"The Lord is my light and my salvation; whom shall I fear? . . . I believe I shall see the goodness of the Lord in the land of the living."

Psalm 42:1-5a

"Why are you cast down, O my soul, and why are you disquieted within me? Hope in God . . . myself and my God."

Psalm 46:1-7

"God is our refuge and strength, a very present help in trouble."

Psalm 118

"Out of my distress I called upon the Lord; the Lord answered me and set me free . . . O give thanks to the Lord, for he is good; for his steadfast love endures forever."

Psalm 121

"I lift up my eyes to the hills, from whence does my help come? My help comes from the Lord, who made heaven and earth."

Psalm 130

"Out of the depths I cry to thee, O Lord . . . If thou, O Lord, shouldst mark iniquities, Lord, who could stand? But there is forgiveness with thee, that thou mayest be feared."

Isaiah 25:6-9

"He will swallow up death forever, and the Lord God will wipe away tears from all faces."

Isaiah 61:1-3

"The Spirit of the Lord God is upon me, because the Lord has anointed me to bring good tidings to the afflicted, he has sent me to bind up the brokenhearted."

Matthew 11:28-30

"Come to me, all who labor and are heavy-laden, and I will give you rest. Take my yoke upon you, and learn from me; for I am gentle and lowly in heart and you will find rest for your souls."

John 11:25

"Jesus said to her, 'I am the resurrection and the life; he who believes in me, though he die, yet shall he live.'"

John 14:1-2

"Let not your hearts be troubled, believe in God, believe also in me. In my Father's house are many rooms."

Romans 8:31-35,37-39

"For I am sure that neither death nor life, nor angels, nor principalities, nor things present, nor things to come, nor powers, nor height, nor depth, nor anything else in all creation, will be able to separate us from the love of God in Christ Jesus our Lord."

Romans 14:7-9

"If we live, we live to the Lord, and if we die, we die to the Lord; so then, whether we live or whether we die, we are the Lord's."

1 Corinthians 15:51-57

"But thanks be to God, who gives us the victory through our Lord Jesus Christ."

Philippians 3:20-21

"But our commonwealth is in heaven, and from it we await a Savior, the Lord Jesus Christ, who will change our lowly body to be like his glorious body."

Philippians 4:4-7

"Rejoice in the Lord, always; again I will say, Rejoice ... Have no anxiety about anything, but in everything by prayer and supplication with thanksgiving let your requests be made known to God."

1 John 3:1-2

"We are God's children now; it does not yet appear what we shall be, but we know that when he appears we shall be like him, for we shall see him as he is."

Revelation 21:1-4

"He will dwell with them, and they shall be his people, and God himself will be with them; he will wipe away every tear from their eyes, and death shall be no more, neither shall there be mourning nor crying nor pain any more, for the former things have passed away."

4. Eulogy

An obituary is often read at a funeral. This is basic biographical information about the deceased, date of birth, date of death, next of kin, etc. It tells a little, but not too much. It is usually restricted to the very basic facts and is not very enlightening or uplifting for anyone.

A much better idea is for some friend or relative to give a eulogy, which is, in effect, a greeting on behalf of the family. The purpose of a eulogy is to tell something about the life of the deceased, and to do so with a personal touch. It may cover some of the same information which is in the obituary, but in a more personal way. This is an opportunity to draw some word pictures about the personality and values of the person who has died. The purpose is not to paint a picture of the deceased which is contradictory to the facts, it is not a time set aside for praise, but it is a chance to share the meaning of that life with others. It also provides a forum for a family to express thanks to all those who are joined together at the service, and to those who have reached out in so many ways to them.

There are some things which a eulogy is not meant to be. It is not a time to lavish praise on the person who has died; rather it is meant to highlight the humanity as well as the life story of this loved one. It is not meant to be a sermon, to try to compete or supplant the words of the pastor. It is rather a time just to offer a few words of appreciation for the life that has been lived and the way in which the Christian community has reached out in love.

A eulogy is best done by someone who has at least a minimal acquaintance with public speaking. It is not always easy to get up in front of a rather large gathering in such an emotional setting and express these sentiments. Also, it is best if this person is able to speak without becoming overly emotional. There is nothing wrong with emotion; it is part of the healing process. But it is often more helpful to all who are present if the person giving the eulogy can be under reasonable control. Thus, it probably should not be a member of the immediate family, except under unusual circumstances. The comments should be written ahead of time, and the pastor be consulted on what will be said.

5. Tapes

If the church has the capacity to tape record the funeral service, it should be done. Very often the experience is so numbing to the family that it is hard to comprehend what is taking place and what has been said. Thus, if the service is recorded, it is possible to listen again and again once the emotional climate has changed, when a person is more able to hear what has taken place. It is best if the church does this automatically and then gives a copy of the tape to the family. There should be no charge for this service; it is a gift from the church.

6. Flowers

As stated in an earlier chapter, we recommend strongly that only the flowers given by the immediate family be placed at the front of the church or near the casket. If the family wishes for other flowers to be displayed, the pastor will find other appropriate places. We want to minimize the amount of flowers, and the implications people often draw from the number which are present.

If the funeral service takes place a day or two before Sunday morning, some flowers might be left for Sunday worship. However, if the funeral takes place early in the week, it is best then to have the flowers taken to nursing homes or other places in the community where they can be enjoyed and appreciated. Ideally, they should be rearranged so they are not readily identifiable as funeral bouquets.

7. Bulletins

It is often helpful to have a printed order of service in the form of a bulletin at a funeral service of worship. Some beautiful bulletin covers have been designed which add meaning and inspiration to such an event, and some of these may be kept on hand at the church for such events. Both the bulletins and the printing should be provided to the family at no charge, this again being a part of the ministry of the church.

8. Reception

A reception following the funeral service can be a time of tremendous support and healing. If there is a burial at a cemetery in close proximity to the church, then the reception may be held following this interment. However, if the burial is to be held some distance away, then it would be better to have the reception immediately following the service, so that all who are present might have the opportunity to share comfort, support and love with the family of the deceased.

Most congregations are more than happy to arrange and coordinate any such reception. It is one of the most important things that a community of faith can do for a grieving family, and there are usually many people who are most willing to help. The congregation, if possible, should have some person who is elected or designated to be in charge of such receptions. Then this person can find others to help, including, at times, friends and neighbors of the deceased. There should not be any charge for such a reception; this too is a part of the ministry of the church.

9. The Sermon

Some form of a sermon or meditation should be given at the funeral service. As was mentioned in the chapter on the role of the pastor, it may be one of the most important sermons ever preached. With the large percentage of people from outside of the congregation in attendance, it is a wonderful time for witnessing to the Gospel and the saving message of Jesus Christ. Examples of funeral sermons are given in the chapters titled "A Story of Death" and "Suicide".

A STORY OF DEATH AND THE ABSENCE OF A WILL

*M*y father received a phone call late one evening informing him that Eva Jean had died. This news was not a complete surprise; Eva Jean was quite elderly and had been in failing health. My father had met Eva Jean more than 40 years earlier. Her mother was a first cousin of his grandmother's, making her about a third cousin.

Eva Jean had lived a rather eccentric and unpredictable life. She had sung in the Metropolitan Opera at one point, and still in her own mind was somewhat of a star. She had gone through five husbands on her journey through life, but at the end was living alone. In addition, she had published a nationally known cookbook and was in the process of compiling information for a sequel to that. In her later years, however, it was clear she was living more and more in a fantasy world, imagining that great wealth was just about to come her way. Then suddenly, one day she died.

Several of her friends called my father and insisted that he come to Dallas to take care of all the arrangements for the funeral. There was no other immediate family, and someone had to do it. This was the last thing my father wished to do, or had the time or money to do, but one of Eva Jean's friends begged and begged by stating, "Eva Jean wanted you to be called if something happened to her, so you must come." Out of a sense of obligation and realization that someone had to do it, he agreed to go.

Before leaving, he called Eva Jean's attorney who was in New York City. The attorney informed him that Eva Jean had left no will. Some of her friends back in Dallas insisted that she had indeed written a will, and this attorney had it in his possession, but of course there was no way to verify this claim. The attorney denied all knowledge of this.

So on Tuesday morning, my father left for Dallas. The funeral director met him at the airport and shared with him all of the information that was presently available. Eva Jean had been out walking her dog on Saturday evening, had suffered a stroke and died almost immediately. Her body had been taken to a nearby funeral home, and now some decisions needed to be made about all of the arrangements. Welcome to Dallas.

However, a lot was happening on several fronts. When my father first came to the apartment where Eva Jean had lived, the phone rang off the hook. Sometimes there were mysterious voices at the other end of the line, sometimes no one would speak. Other friends descended on the apartment, giving much advice about what should be done, a good deal of it contradictory. It was apparent that some of the "friends" had already searched the apartment before he arrived. One of them later came to him with two diamond rings she had taken, for in her words, she "didn't want anyone else to steal them."

My father began looking through some of the papers in the apartment, searching for a possible will, but found mountains of other kinds of materials instead. There were stacks and stacks of old love letters from various suitors, some of them former husbands. Also piled high in the apartment were thousands of recipes, gathered to prepare for another book.

Shortly after his arrival, two women showed up at the apartment, each with an attorney in tow, each of them looking for a will. On a later afternoon, both of these women, with attorneys, showed up at the First State Bank to study the contents of the safety deposit box. However, they happened to arrive at the same time, and a lot of shouting ensued between them, almost to the point of a fistfight.

My father then was asked to go to the funeral home to make the necessary arrangements. He brought with him two of Eva Jean's finest dresses for the burial. But the female funeral director just looked at him with disdain. "You are not going to bury her in one of those, are you?"

"What should we bury her in?" asked my father.

"We bury women in nightgowns," said the undertaker. "It shows that they are just sleeping." Of course, the funeral home just happened to have a rather extensive display of silk nightgowns.

A problem was emerging. A funeral and all of the extras cost money, and it was not at all clear who was going to pay for all of this. There was no indication that Eva Jean had any financial resources at all; she may have been destitute. Looking through her personal correspondence my father found all sorts of fantastic dreams about riches and wealth, but they seemed to be more fantasy than reality.

He then made an attempt to find some other relatives. In the Dallas phone book there were several people with the same last name, so he called them. None of them admitted to being a relative. Finally, he found the name of a relatives in a notebook in the desk, and called this man on the phone. Sure enough, he was a closer relatives than my father, so this was exactly the right person to find. However, he said he was just leaving on a trip to Europe and would not be able to come. He told my father to just take care of everything.

Upon returning to the apartment, the strange phone calls continued. One call was from St. Louis, from a person who identified herself as "Eva Jean's dearest and closest friend". This woman insisted that Eva Jean should be cremated; this is what she had wanted. My father told her that he had already been to the funeral home and made other arrangements. But the woman was adamant and said, "If you do not have her cremated, I will make big trouble for you."

My father didn't know what to make of this, so he asked her what kind of trouble she was going to make. The woman said that she didn't know yet, but she was arriving on the plane the next day for the funeral, and by then would certainly think of something. So my father checked on cremation, and in finding it to be less expensive, changed the plans and cancelled the burial arrangements. He was not about to get into some kind of confrontation with Eva Jean's "closest and dearest friend".

On Wednesday morning he tried to find a lawyer who would help sort things out. Several calls were fruitless. One of the lawyers contacted went so far as to call the attorney in New York, checking out all of the information, but then he also refused. Now my father didn't know what to do. He had no legal help, no money forthcoming, no other family members to consult, and a funeral scheduled for that afternoon. At the same time, there were several of these elderly women hovering around the apartment, clamoring for attention.

The funeral took place on Wednesday afternoon at the funeral home. My father, who is a pastor, decided to just go ahead and officiate at the service himself. He wrote a funeral sermon and planned the Scripture passages and music. Some 20 to 25 people were there for the service. He now wished he could get on the next plane and return home.

In many ways, though, he was just beginning. The apartment was just filled with possessions, and no one would help sort this all out. Finally, he called a pastor friend of his in the city, a seminary classmate, and asked if he knew a good attorney. He recommended one in his congregation by the name of Fred Smith, and my father called him. The attorney suggested that nothing more be done until he could come and visit him on Thursday morning. My father wanted to go home, but he agreed to wait.

On Thursday the attorney and my father met to dispose of the property. After the attorney departed, one woman knocked at the door and claimed that Eva Jean had said she could have her dog. My father replied, "Wonderful. Take him." Another came and said that she had been promised the large bird, a parrot, which made incessant noise, so my father told her to quickly take it away.

Another woman kept showing up at the door, and when my father tried to discourage this activity, she said that she had a pair of shoes she had lent to Eva Jean. My father then went into the midst of a huge closet with at least a hundred pairs of shoes and found a pair she described. She had also told him she had a girdle in there. Then my father discovered there was a whole roomful of girdles, some of them brand new. He told her she could have them all. It wasn't long before the woman reappeared and said that the sewing machine and frying pan were also hers, and my father also gave them to her gladly.

The apartment was jammed to the rafters. Eva Jean had never thrown away anything. In her final year of life, she had apparently just decided to use only the living room. Every other room was filled. There were closets of dresses and shoes and memorabilia from her days in the opera. She had walls lined with artwork and recipes. In the kitchen and storage areas were hundreds of old jars, kitchen food stuffs, broken dishes, etc. She also had numerous drawers filled with pills and cosmetics.

On Friday morning he hired a huge pickup truck which had high sideboards for more room. His pastor friend came over and helped load the stuff to cart it away. The truck was filled before even a fraction of the possessions was taken out of the apartment. At one time they stacked a pile of dresses all the way to the ceiling, then another stack of opera clothes, and another pile of old purses, shoes, and hats. These were given to the lodge where Eva Jean had belonged.

This process went on most of Friday, and by 4:30 when the attorney arrived, they had only removed a small portion of the stuff. My father wanted to go home. He was tired, he had work to do, he wanted to see his family, and his expenses were mounting. There was no guarantee that any of these out-of-pocket costs would be reimbursed. But he agreed to stay a bit longer to help the attorney settle some matters.

Just about this time, the attorney received information that the cremation could not take place. They needed a document with my father's signature on it, also that of the attorney; and of a notary public, before it would be allowed. This entailed a frantic rush hour journey cross-town to the funeral home to sign the burial permits. Fortunately, the pastor friend was willing to give him a ride.

The attorney then suggested that he just hire a truck to come and haul all of the rest of the stuff away. The attorney would then store all of the inventoried items until he was advised about the distribution of them by the close relatives. My father was greatly relieved and decided to leave for home on the first plane.

The scenario did not end with his departure from town, however. He checked back periodically with the attorney, but this man would tell him nothing. He tried again to call the attorney in New York, but he would not return the calls. My father tried to regain some of his costs, but no one would tell him if there were any assets to be used for this. It continued to be a very frustrating experience and large expense.

At the same time, my father was told by some who had been close to Eva Jean that she owned some valuable property near Chicago. For all he knew, Eva Jean might have been wealthy, but with no one telling him anything, there was not much that could be done. He also found out later that Eva Jean had wanted her ashes sent to a cemetery in Chicago to be buried with her parents, but he could never find out whether this had been actually carried out.

He gave his pastor friend some electric blankets for his help, as well as an antique mirror. They later told my father that they had to take the mirror for refinishing; it had been full of termites. There was also a baby grand in the apartment, so the attorney hired a truck to haul this piano, together with some furniture, to his secretary's home. He also took Eva Jean's car. My father never could discover whether any of these items were eventually disbursed to family members.

As bizarre as this story may sound, there are parts of this which are not all that unusual. Let me draw some conclusions from this episode that can be directed to all of us.

1. To die without a will is really a very foolish thing to do. Rather, we should say that to live without a will is not very wise. It can create havoc and disruption in the lives of those who are left.

2. When there is no will, conflict is almost inevitable among those who survive.

3. Funeral homes can be helpful, but the meter is running, and the costs can appreciate quickly.

4. Attorneys have tremendous power when there is no will and no executor of the estate. Also, not all attorneys are completely trustworthy.

5. Large sums or small sums of money from an estate can just vanish into thin air, unless there exists some systematic plan for the distribution of the assets.

ESTATE PLANNING

*T*he story of death in the previ-
ous chapter is a rather outlandish example of the confusion that
reigns when there is a lack of planning. However, even in more
normal situations, if there has been no adequate planning, some
degree of chaos and disruption will be almost inevitable. We each
have an estate, and we have a very definite choice, whether we
wish it to be allocated the way we want it to be, or whether we will
just "shake the dice" and let things fall where they will.

Estate planning begins with the realization that when we are
no longer living on this earth, our possessions will still be here.
There are all kinds of comments about taking it with us. Some of
them are humorous and others of them seem to have some
measure of seriousness about it. Obviously though, everything we
have will still be here when we are not. More important, all that we
have will then belong to someone else. It seems as if we should
have our say about who that someone else will be.

The term "estate planning" refers simply to the creation of a
very definite plan for the disbursement and distribution of all that
we own, both for the present and for the future. It is far more than
just a financial document; in a sense it will reflect our basic values
in life, our priorities, and even our faith. We must give this estate
plan a thoughtful and prayerful consideration as soon as possible.

No danger exists from doing this plan too early in life; a substantial danger exists in waiting until it is too late.

1. Avoidance of Taxes

There is always one fundamental principle that we should keep in mind when we look at financial and estate planning. The goal of such preparation is not somehow to "get the government". We may feel that way at times, and obviously many of us have strong reservations about the way the government uses its revenues. The basic principles involved in estate planning is this: the tax structure of our country has been designed and implemented in order to accomplish some definite and specific goals. Some of these goals are financial, and others are social. In other words, the government has established policies to encourage certain kinds of charitable giving, and to discourage other kinds of financial decisions. It does this in order to create a better and more humane society.

The government has determined over the period of years that it is extremely important for various charities in our midst to be adequately funded, because these groups provide tremendous service and support that could not be duplicated by the government or anyone else. If these charities did not have sufficient funding, the government would then be forced to try and meet these needs in other ways. And it is abundantly clear to most observers that independent charities can provide for these social needs much more efficiently and in a more humane fashion than can a large central governmental system.

So when we look at estate planning, our major goal is not to cheat the government out of something which is rightfully public money. We wish to pay our fair share of taxes, to return a portion of what we have accumulated to our nation, which has given us the opportunity to gather these assets. At the same time, however, we do not wish to pay more of our estate in taxes than is needed.

We should rather direct a substantial part of our estate toward meeting the needs of the various charitable organizations, than to just give by default ot the government. The tax laws were established for this very reason, and we are being good citizens by helping the government carry out the social, political and charitable agenda of our nation. When we respond to the incentives which ahve been established by the leaders, when we utilize the tax structure to give more to charitable causes, then we are indeed being faithful to our country and to our own values.

2. Needs in Estate Planning

There are three areas to be addresses when we begin to do estate planning. Each of these must be considered as a part of the whole.

1. We consider our own financial needs for the rest of our life. We will want, as much as possible, to provide an adequate income for ourselves for the rest of our working years, as well as after we retire. Thus, we will wish to invest our assets as wisely as possible, so we can maximize all we have. Part of our planning process needs to look at ways we can decrease our current and future taxes, so that we will have as much as possible available for our own use and for others.

2. We consider the needs of our families. We want to leave those persons closest to us sufficient financial resources to provide for them and protect them after our own death. We want to share with our family members in death as we have in life; this is part of our love and commitment to them. There is a whole range of creative options available for consideration in providing our family's essential resources.

3. We consider the needs of others, of the many worthwhile charitable organizations in our midst. Christians will wish to demonstrate the same priorities of giving and sharing in death which they evidenced in life. Again, there are some creative ways of giving which can benefit us and our families (the first two goals) when we are still alive, while at the same time providing inestimable help to charities of our choice. Our local congregation, various community agencies, church colleges, seminaries, national church bodies and many other such ministries are all admirable recipients of this kind of giving.

Wills

Without a doubt, the first step in estate planning is to create a will. Anyone who does not have a will in this day and age is playing a dangerous game of roulette with the future. As was emphasized in earlier chapters, to not have a will is a way of avoiding reality and is contrary to all that we know about Christian stewardship. Those who insist on going through life without a will are leaving their families extremely vulnerable and letting the government make many decisions that should rightfully belong to each of us. I would strongly hope that this book would encourage and motivate each reader to move quickly and carefully to draw up a will.

For those who have not written a will (an estimated 70% of people who died in the United States in a recent year did not have a will), it might be helpful or frightening to know that the state in which you reside already has a will for you. You probably don't know what is in it. You haven't read it, approved it or signed it, but it is there for all those who die without a will. The government has set up the mechanism to decide who gets everything you have, your investments, your children, and all of your property. Isn't that comforting?

A will is called the last will and testament. Another way of stating this is to call it our final testimony. This testimony should have something to do with our faith in Jesus Christ, with our basic understanding of life. A testimony of our values should be proclaimed in our wills.

The will offers us an opportunity to continue what we have been doing, to give in death just as we have given in life. It may be that you wish to give generously to the local congregation where you have been nurtured, blessed and loved. You may even wish to continue the tithe you have given over the years. Some will wish to give more, others less than the biblical 10%. It is important that we consider all of the alternatives that are open to us and create a will which reflects our basic and most fundamental Christian beliefs.

The American Lutheran Church has created a tract entitled "What Is a Will?" which gives several excellent reasons why we should have a will.

1. *A will is about living and caring.* It is a message for the living, to be for the living. In most cases, it can be changed at any time.

2. *A will brings order and direction to the estate.* Making a will takes thought and prompts us to evaluate our possessions. We may discover that our estate is worth more than we had previously thought, not an uncommon discovery. Are there possessions which should be distributed to certain persons? Who is going to receive the estate? All of these questions must be faced as we prepare a will.

3. *A will may preserve the value of our possession.* The decisions reflected in the will should clear the way for the prompt and inexpensive transfer of these possessions to others. If we die without a will, the state will distribute this property. In addition, court costs and taxes are usually much higher in the absence of a will and reduce the amount which can be given to heirs or charity.

4. *A will protects children and other dependents.* Through the will a person may name the individual or couple who would serve as replacement parents. The importance of this determination is not hard to understand. For minor children, or for any dependent family member, a guardian is chosen who would truly give loving care, who would be the best for this situation. At the same time the will may also provide for the costs of the basic care of these dependents, as well as education and other needs. Of course, the will also provides for the final disposition of the estate to the children when they will best be able to handle the responsibility.

5. *A will personalizes the transfer of possessions.* Only through a will is it possible to design the transfers of personal goods, heirlooms, furnishings, collectables and other possessions. The lifelong friend who has shared a hobby or other interest with you, the child who would truly treasure the pocket watch, the tools or ring, the charity whose ministry you admire — none can benefit from your estate without a will. Personalizing a last gift of your possessions speaks of your caring to those who will rejoice in the life you have lived.

6. *A will provides for charitable gifts.* Most persons have some favorite charities which are deemed worthy to receive generous bequests. Any possession may be transferred to a qualified nonprofit organization through a will. By law, charitable transfers reduce the amount of the taxable estate.

7. *A will may prevent family conflicts and anxiety.* The will provides direction and clearly states the wishes. Those who survive and have the responsibility of settling the estate are much better equipped to do so with specific instructions in a will. This should minimize conflict, confusion, struggles over decisions and family disruption by documenting the exact desires and plans of the deceased.

8. *A will may design a financial plan for loved ones.* The will can be structured to provide installment gifts or benefits. Regular income payments can be designated for a spouse or other heirs. A total gift may be divided so that payments are given to an individual or an organization in installments over a period of years. The will can create a plan which will pay income for life to those who are named, and the rest can be given to charity, accomplishing several objectives through one plan.

Once the decisions is made to create a will, then it is important to know what should be contained in that will. The following are some suggestions for the kind for the kind of information that should be secured for the visit to an attorney:

1. Social Security numbers.
2. Date and place of birth.
3. Information on marriage and any previous marriages.
4. Income tax information.
5. Health status.
6. Information on children, including education goals.
7. Information on both sets of grandparents, and both sets of brothers and sisters.
8. Any money that might be inherited.
9. Armed forces record, serial number and dates of service.
10. A list of bank accounts, savings certificates, treasury bonds, money market accounts, stocks and bonds, includ-

ing the purchase price, date purchased, present market value and how the asset is titled.

11. Mortgage and market value information on your home and and how the asset is titled.

12. Complete information on other property owned and how the asset is titled.

13. Complete information, including policy number, of all insurance policies.

14. Balance sheets and profit-loss statement of any business you might own.

15. Whether you have ever lived in a state with a commuity property law.

16. Copies of pension plans, benefits and stock options.

17. Title information for automobiles.

18. A list of other major possessions: boats, trailers, china, art, family heirlooms, copyrights, patents, etc.

19. A list of debts.

20. Any safe deposit vaults that are held and the location of other important documents.

21. An accounting of any substantial gifts made in the past.

22. Names and addresses of the first and second choices for guardian of minor children and for estate representative or executor.

23. Any special arrangements for funeral arrangements, burial, or organ donation.

24. Any special provisions that would result in the children being treated other than equally.

Now it is time to turn to a discussion of charitable giving. There are so many creative and exciting ways to give at the present time, but most of us are unable to sort out all of this information. Inestimable sums of money are lost to worthwhile charities simply because people do not have sufficient awareness of the options available, and because they have not taken the initiative to learn what these might be. It should be almost essential for Christians to do everything possible to give, to find all of those creative methods and opportunities to provide for the work of ministry after we are gone. Much of the following will be an introduction to this whole area of giving.

4. Effective Charitable Giving

Effective charitable giving involves several aspects.

Giving the *right amount*. This can be determined best by understanding all of the necessary information about the size and scope of the estate, and what some of the alternatives for giving might be.

Giving at the *right time*. Timing is important in many areas of life, not the least in the area of giving. Again, this depends in large part on knowing something about charitable giving.

Giving in the *best way*. The following information is to suggest some ways this might be accomplished.

Now and Later

There are two basic times to give, now and later. Those gifts which are best given at this time include:

Antiques	Livestock
Art work	Life insurance
Business inventories	Mortgages
Collections of value	Notes and leases
Crops	Real estate
Jewelry	Royalties
Land contracts	Stocks and bonds

When making a gift of stock which has increased in value and has been owned longer than the legally required holding period, it is better to give this gift outright, rather than trying to sell and give the proceeds. By giving outright, the tax on capital gains is avoided, and a charitable deduction is given for the fair market value of the stock.

However, when giving a stock which has decreased in value, consider selling it and then giving the cash proceeds. This makes it possible to establish a capital loss which can offset other capital gain, or to some extent, even offset ordinary income tax.

There are many ways to *give later.* Some of these include:

A. Life Insurance

There are many ways to use life insurance to make a gift to a charitable organization. Here are some which are the most popular.

1. Purchase a policy which designates a charity as the irrevocable owner and beneficiary. By paying a relatively small annual premium, one might guarantee a rather large future gift. The premiums are tax deductible.

It is also possible for a person to make a one-time payment on a universal life policy, which will purchase a death benefit.

For example: Bill and Sharon are in their mid-30s. They have two children. This year they have a combined taxable income of $45,000, which means they were liable for $9,508 in federal income taxes. Their church recently established a foundation. Bill and Sharon decided to make a $5,000 gift to this foundation, which reduced their federal income tax bill by $1,650. However, they decided to split the gift. A thousand dollars in cash was given directly to the foundation. The other $4,000 was used to purchase an insurance contract on Sharon's life. A one-time payment is made on a universal life insurance policy, which purchases a $50,000 death benefit.

2. Change the beneficiary (the person or organization receiving the policy) to a charity. The charity can either be the beneficiary or co-beneficiary (shared with others).

3. Add the name of a charity to the list of the beneficiaries on a policy that is already owned, in case the other beneficiaries do not survive you.

4. Give a paid-up policy outright and deduct its replacement value.

For example: Jim and Joan are 50 years old and have a paid-up $25,000 life insurance policy, with a cash value of $15,000. They decide to give this policy to their church, thus realizing a $15,000 income tax deduction.

The church receives the dividends and has the use of the cash value of the policy. At the time of Jim and Joan's death, the church receives the $25,000 death benefit.

5. Assign annual dividends from policies to the congregation as a regular means of giving tax-free income, which is deductible.

B. Give real estate, but keep it.

This is called the life estate agreement. It allows a person to make a charitable gift of a personal residence or farm, and retain the right to live there and use the property and its income for life.

Example 1: Oscar is 63 years old. His wife died several years before and he has not remarried. His two children are grown and have families of their own. Oscar has an annual income which puts him in the 50% tax bracket. His total estate is $750,000. The value of his home is $150,000.

Oscar has decided to give a remainder interest in his home to his congregation. He can then live in his home for as long as he lives. His lifestyle will not change at all, but he has saved the following:

1. He saves income tax savings of almost $22,000, realized immediately.

2. He had a potential real estate tax savings of $55,500. (By leaving the remainder interest in his home to his church, he has removed a $150,000 asset from his estate.)

If Oscar wishes to put that $150,000 back into his estate for his children, he could use a portion of the income tax savings to purchase life insurance.

Example 2. Dave and Eileen, both in their late 40s, have a combined estate valued at $1.2 million. Dave grew up on a farm which he now owns, inherited from his parents. He rents some of the land to a local farmer. The farm is worth $300,000. If Dave and Eileen would die in 1985, they would pay federal estate taxes of $146,000. This would leave their children with $1,054,000.

However, they decided in Dave's will that upon his death the $300,000 farm will pass into a testamentary charitable remainder trust, with a church college as a beneficiary. This reduces the estate taxes by $112,000, and the trust will pay Eileen $24,000 a year for as long as she lives.

C. Ways to Give and Receive

There are many ways to arrange such a gift. Most of these are based on giving money or property to a charity, receiving the income earned by the assets invested (and in some cases a part of the principal), and designating what remains to be a gift at death. This is a way of arranging to give money or property after it is no longer needed. *Some examples:*

1. Charitable Remainder Annuity Trust

Ruth is 70 years old and a widow. Her annual income is $25,000 from Social Security and some investments. She is in the 30% tax bracket. She has $100,000 in common stock purchased many years before for $20,000. The yield on this stock has been about 4% per year. Ruth is unhappy about the earnings, but knows she would have to pay capital gains of $9,600 if she sold the stock. She wants her children to receive as much as possible.

Ruth's current estate is valued at $500,000. If she died in 1985, the federal estate tax bill would be $59,500, leaving her children about $440,000.

Ruth decided to give the $100,000 in stock to her church, in a charitable remainder annuity trust. She will then be paid an income of $10,000 a year from this trust for as long as she lives. This more than doubles her current rate of return, and she avoids capital gains altogether.

Ruth also receives a current income tax deduction based on the value of the church's remainder interest. This is valued at $39,478, so she has an income tax savings of $11,843.

By placing the $100,000 of stock in a charitable remainder, she removes the asset from her estate. This results in an estate tax savings of $34,000.

If Ruth wishes to place that $100,000 back into her estate, she can use a portion of her added income to buy life insurance.

2. Charitable Gift Annuity

Ernest is 60 years old and single. He wishes to give a gift to his church, but also wants to receive an annual income from this gift.

Thus, he gave a gift of $20,000 to the church, and will receive a lifetime annuity of $1,400 a year. He also realizes an income tax deduction of $9,743, and receives a portion of each annuity payment tax free.

3. Charitable Lead Trust

Kathy is 55 years old and has an estate worth two million dollars. If she died in 1985, her estate taxes would be $659,000. So Kathy decided to put $500,000 into a charitable remainder trust, with the annual income to her church of $50,000.

She has saved $191,550 in estate taxes. Her daughter then will receive what is in the trust after 20 years.

If Kathy would place one million dollars into the lead trust, the church would receive $100,000 a year, and her estate tax savings would increase to $374,000.

4. A Charitable Remainder Unitrust, for College Expenses

Mark and Margie have three teenage children. Mark's income puts him in the 50% marginal tax bracket. He owns stocks with a market value of $60,000, which he purchased for $20,000. Their oldest child starts college in another year. Selling the stock to pay for college is an option, but that would mean a capital gains tax of $8,000.

Instead, Mark and Margie decided to give the $60,000 in stock to a 20-year charitable remainder unitrust. Now the family receives a 7% income flow from the trust each year for 20 years, which can be used for college expenses for their children. At the end of the 20 years the gift can go to a college, a local congregation, or other charity.

Because this was a gift, there were no capital gains. Also they received a charitable income tax deduction worth $14,054 in the year of gift. There was a steady income flow to the children in college, depending on the interest rates, and this income paid to the children was taxed in their tax brackets.

5. Philanthropic Retirement

(The children are grown.)

Roe and Bev are age 50. Roe is a self-employed owner of a small business. He is in the 50% tax bracket. He and Bev wish to prepare for retirement as well as do something for the church. So they set up a charitable remainder unitrust in the name of the congregation.

From age 50 to age 65, they can put up to 50% of their income into the unitrust. At age 65, they can begin receiving annual payments of up to 10% of the value of the trust, which can be tax free. At death the remainder of the trust will go to the church.

This allows Roe and Bev to shelter up to 50% of their income. Some of the savings could be used to purchase life insurance in a wealth replacement trust, so heirs would receive a comparable amount.

In summary, there are many unique and creative options to consider when it comes to estate planning. It is best to consult with someone who both understands the law and the options available in the area of charitable giving. Many tax attorneys, accountants and financial planners understand a great deal about the law, but do not know much about the opportunities for charitable giving. In many cases, they will even discourage such giving. Thus, it is important to find someone to help who has a basic awareness of Christian giving.

Congregations should also find people who can intentionally encourage others to consider the church in the creation of the estate plan. Many financial advisors do not include the church in the estate simply because they never thought about it; no one mentioned this possibility. A congregation should think about having a Development Committee or a Foundation Board which can seek to inform and educate the members about charitable giving. It often takes many years before this work can bear fruit for the church, but it certainly is a part of our stewardship responsibility. In addition, it obviously offers unbelievable possibilities to the congregation for gifts to fund future ministry.

A LIVING
LEGACY

*M*odern technology has given us many new opportunities for communicating with each other and with future generations. One of the most amazing advances has come in the form of video tape. Now we can put on such a tape the important memories we want to leave our children and grandchildren. We can actually give to future generations the lasting gift of a video tape. In the past there are some who have created audio tapes of special occasions, or who have taped the voice of a loved one, but the new possibilities in the area of media are far superior to that which was available in the past.

Consider the following story. A man has just found out that he has a malignant turmor. There is no question that this man and his family will pray continuously for the miracle of healing, as well as securing all of the possible treatments. The entire support system will help in any way possible. No one will give up hope that this illness might be reversed.

At the same time, there is also a possibility that this man may not have long to live on this earth. Depending upon the location of the cancer, and the type of malignancy, there may even be a low probability of survival. In addition, because of the illness, there is also the reality that the man's health may deteriorate rather quickly. It then becomes clear to all of his loved ones that many people may never have the opportunity to see him, particularly future grandchildren or others who are too young to remember.

It so happens that this man's church has recently purchased some video equipment. It is then suggested to this man and his family that he come to the church at his convenience and make a tape for his family. This is what happens: the camera is turned on and the man talks for an hour or two about his life, his values and faith, his family, his hopes for his children and his grandchildren. All of this is recorded on video tape, which can be played on any video cassette recorder. It then becomes a living legacy.

Pastor Richard Nelson of our church staff did just such a thing with his 85-year-old mother. He suggested to her that the family would very much appreciate it if she would give the gift of a living legacy to them, one that could be seen by her children and grandchildren, and their children yet to be. His mother was very hesitant to be interviewed on camera, her experience with cameras having been mainly with the box camera of long ago. She was uncertain about whether she would know what to say, or know the answers to the questions which were asked, and if she would remember things past. She would have "preferred not to". But through some gentle encouragement, telling her that she would hardly be aware of the presence of the camera, she changed her mind and was willing to go through with it.

Pastor Richard set the tone for the interview by talking informally before the camera was started, explaining some of the events which would be discussed and telling his mother that it would be a fun time. He encouraged her to "relax and enjoy". At the beginning of the tape, Richard gave some introductory comments, describing the goals of this tape and some of the aspects to be discussed.

He then gave his mother's full name, her date of birth, her marriage date, and mentioned that, though his father had died some seven years earlier, they would include him in their conversation, so that he too would be a part of this legacy to be passed down to the family. Then Richard mentioned each of the children, date of birth and marriage, so that, when the video was viewed, all of the family members would hear themselves mentioned.

His mother began by remembering her early childhood. She repeated some information Richard had never heard before, as she talked about her own mother and father. She described how they had come from different parts of Norway, one from a very poor family background, the other from a family that was quite well to do. She told about how this marriage was so contrary to the custom of that time. In Norway the poor married the poor and the upper class married those of similar background. Here in America, though, things were different, and this turned out to be a very good marriage.

She went on to share information about an uncle who had been born on the way to this country. We sometimes think that we are a mobile people today, but very often people were much more so a century ago. Richard discovered that his mother's parents moved more times than he has ever moved. From Iowa they went to South Dakota, and when they feared some Indian neighbors, they went to North Dakota, then to Minnesota, and finally back to Iowa. This was all done by train or horse and buggy.

His mother talked about her wedding and the pouring rain she remembered, the lightning and thunder so ferocious that they all had to sit on their chairs and wait for the storm to finish before concluding the ceremony. Richard's father came to life in the conversation, when she explained the way they had met at a youth convention. His father's parents had invited three girls to stay at their home during the conference, and his mother was one of these.

Later his father was drafted into World War I, but before he left he asked one of the young ladies who had stayed at his parents' home to write him letters when he was gone. He also gave her a friendship ring. When he returned from the war, they were engaged, married, and started out on the home farm as his father was dying of cancer.

As the interview unfolded, Richard's mother became less aware of the camera and more interested in talking about her children. Richard had been born in a farm home during a December snowstorm, his grandmother assisting at the birth. The doctor never did arrive. His mother talked about the time Richard had been lost in a cornfield, and the family and neighbors searched for many hours before he was found.

She told about Richard's father's decision to sell the farm and become a minister, and to attend Luther Theological Seminary in St. Paul. She told her son for the first time ever how upset she had been with his decision to give up farming for the ministry, and how she "cried for weeks". But eventually she supported this decision, and told about her life as the wife of a pastor. In the remainder of this part she described the various places in which his father served.

After a break of several minutes, the second part of the interview commenced. This was primarily a time of show and tell. The family Bible was opened, and the center section explored, the place where the family records were contained. The camera took a close-up of his father's birth and baptismal certificates, as well as his parents' wedding certificate. Then there was a look at the information about each of the children, each one's birth and baptism and marriage. the next part recorded their conversation about the death of Richard's father. They talked about the love and nurture that had been present for the familly at this time of sorrow.

Richard then held up a copy of the Norwegian songbook and the small hymnbook his mother had given to him at his confirmation. Several other books were displayed—*Hurlburt's Bible Story*, which his mother had just read cover to cover, plus the book *Giants in the Earth*, describing the life of the early immigrants. A copy of the *Lutheran Standard* magazine with the cover of poverty in Ethiopia led his mother to express her concern for what should be done for the hungry in the world, and her desire to help in this effort. They also displayed copies of *Time* magazine, the local newspaper, and a letter that his mother had received in the mail that day. This section was meant to convey to her family her strong love of reading and interest in the world situations of today.

His mother also talked about her Christian faith. She emphasized several times how valuable it had been for her to memorize Bible passages and Luther's *Small Catechism* in her early days, and how she still remembers a good deal of this. She also displayed her new Easter hat she had purchased, and talked about what this meant to her.

An afghan also was filmed, and Richard's mother explained that she had made 25 of these, which had been given to her children and grandchildren. Richard and his mother ended the interview by singing together the "Doxology". The final picture was a painting from Norway, showing that the past was a part of the present, and would be with them as they moved into the future. Richard closed by giving his mother a hug and by saying thank you to her.

The above is an illustration of what a living legacy might be like. Different alternatives would be available, depending primarily on the interests and priorities of the people involved. The following are some suggestions for people who might wish to record such a legacy. Many additional questions and issues might spin off from these, but this can provide the framework.

I. Early Years

A. Recollections of grandparents, parents, brothers and sisters, other relatives and acquaintances.
1. Personalities and characteristics, hereditary traits.
2. Family stores about these.
3. Human interest details not found in written family records.
B. Family circumstances surrounding the birth of the person interviewed.
C. Locations of family homes, why they moved, etc.
D. Any pre-school memories.
E. Education: grade school—building, teachers, friends, transportation; high school—courses and achievements, sports, clubs, offices; fads during growing years.
F. Medical practices, dental work, surgery, etc., or experience with major epidemics.
G. Pranks and humorous experiences.
H. Jobs and work experiences.
I. Teenage years.
1. Social life: dances, dating, music, movies, summer outings

2. Influential teachers, other models during formative years.

3. Special friends.

4. Feelings about this time of life.

5. Special lessons in music, art, dance, etc.

6. Hobbies, special interests, pets.

7. Vacation and travel.

J. Faith.

    1. Religious activities, attendance at church, youth groups, classes; again, influential teachers or pastors.

    2. Religious experiences, influences, reading.

K. Family and community.

    1. Family members, brothers and sisters, characteristics.

    2. Child-rearing philosophy of the parents, family roles.

    3. Outstanding qualities of the father, mother, children.

    4. Religious practices in the home.

    5. Houses lived in, neighborhoods, neighbors.

    6. Financial status of the family.

    7. Difficulties faced by the family.

    8. Nature of the community, town, city, farm where the family lived — size, landmarks, traditions, population, etc.

II. Adult Years

A. Military service: why entered, what branch, feelings at the time of entry, basic training, specialized training, promotions, honors, combat duty, friendships, social life, conflicts.

B. Post-high-school experience.

    1. Motivation: decision not to or to attend college or technical school, why or why not.

    2. Schools attended, why selected, how financed.

    3. Subjects studied, major interests.

    4. Social life, activities, dating.

    5. Degree and honors; if dropped out, why.

    6. Unusual learning experiences, influential teachers and friends.

    7. Religious activities, experiences, conflicts.

C. Vocations and career.

    1. What careers and why.

2. Changes and promotions, transfers, retraining.
3. Important positions held, success and failure.
4. Effect of job on family, how job was done.
5. Membership in professional organizations, union or business group.
6. Unusual experiences.

III. Marriage and Family

A. Courtship and marriage.
B. Characteristics of the children as they grew: differences, habits, character, talents, hobbies, humorous incidents, problems, joys, sorrows.
C. Houses lived in, neighbors, close family friends, effects of moves on the family.
D. Role of spouse and yourself in the home; the philosophy of child rearing; daily routine, transportation, radio, magazines, TV, garden.
E. Family traditions, vacations, birthdays, graduations, religious practices.
F. Adult medical experiences.
G. Religious participations.
H. Social and civic activities, politics, PTA, clubs.
I. Personal traits: best abilities, physical handicaps, preferences and dislikes — food, music, books, art, radio, movies, TV.
J. Memorable travels.
K. Impact of retirement: financial, family, friends.
L. Historic events: Depression, emigration, family history, world wars, natural disasters.
M. Changes seen through lifetime: technology, fashions, mass media, morality, politics, diet.
N. Greatest joys and sorrows, most important contributions, major turning points.
O. What counsel to give for the new generation, how to live successfully.

IV. Folklore Items

This can either be a part of the regular interview, or the topic may become the basis for a separate interview.

A. Superstitions, what brings bad luck or good, nature signs that predict rain or snow, bad winters, warm summers.

B. Home cures, remedies about such problems as hiccups, warts, coughs, toothaches, colds, arthritis, birth control.

C. Legends and tall tales common to the area or to a particular job.

D. Traditional customs for celebrating weddings, births, birthdays, April Fool Day, Valentines Day, Halloween, May Day, Memorial Day, funerals.

E. Childhood rhymes, ditties, and games.

F. Nicknames of schoolmates, work companions.

Beyond simply telling these things, the person being interviewed might visually show some of the following: forgotten or obliterated roads, buildings, gravesites, boundary lines, canals, trails, and other historical spots. A portable camera is necessary for this.

Also, a person might explain or demonstrate how to do things like foodmaking, baking, canning, meat drying, herb teas, etc. In addition the person may show how to do arts and crafts, old-time fences, clothes, pindolls, card tricks, soapmaking, pottery, braiding, weaving, quilting, and whittling.

He or she may also perform, sing or play old folk songs or music, quote poetry or readings.

V. Genealogical Information

Clarify the family relationships needed, and obtain such useful genealogical information as full names, names of all members in each family unit, and dates and locations of births, baptisms, dedications, marriages and deaths.

A Possible Format

Some questions to ask a person being interviewed:

1. Tell me something about yourself, your family, marriage, and career. What feelings do you have as you talk about each area?

2. As you look back, what are some pleasant and unpleasant things you remember?
3. If you could, are there events in your life you would change? What are they? Can you be specific?
4. How do you feel about your life at this stage?
5. What are your concerns for the future?
6. Do you ever think about dying? How do you feel about it? What meaning or significance does it have for you?
7. Do you have keepsakes, what are they, what do they mean to you? What are you going to do with them? Did you ever think of leaving a legacy? To whom will you leave it? Why? How will you decide who will get it?
8. In general, are you satisfied with the life you have lived?
9. Are there any new things you have done as you have passed 65 that you didn't do earlier?
10. Are there activities you still like to do?
11. How do you feel about the manner in which aging is treated in our society?
12. How has the church served you and your needs?

There are many different directions such an interview may take. Hopefully, this book has created a desire within each reader to act—to leave such a legacy. What a beautiful gift a living legacy, as well as a will, would be for a family when a loved one dies. These gifts would be cherished by their families more than we could ever imagine. They would truly be gifts for the living. In addition, they would signify an acceptance of the reality of death, of the fact that we will not live forever on this earth. I encourage each reader to consider giving such priceless heirlooms.

MOVING ON

$\mathcal{W}$hen death interrupts our family, it is clear that this event will forever change the way we have been living, our relationships, our dreams, our hopes, our future. There is no way to just move on in the same way we have been traveling, with no disruption. Rather, it means instead a significant period of grieving, of adjustment, of working through the grief and then getting on with our lives. We may not want to do this, at least right away, we may try and hang on to our loss and pain for too long. But there comes a time when the right moment appears for us to begin moving on. The purpose of this book has been to help us understand this need, and then to act on it.

I would like to conclude this exposition on the experience of death by suggesting three guideposts, three markers for those who are now in transition. These are meant to be some words of hope and support and encouragement. Everyone grieves differently, but there are some common threads which can be helpful as we move through death to life. Let me suggest the following:

1. This difficult time of change and reorientation can be a time of positive growth and development. We cannot change what has happened to our loved one and to us, but we can change how we respond to what has happened. We are not powerless even during our grieving. This can be a time when we learn a great deal about ourselves, about or own needs and strengths and resources.

It also can be a time when we find some very surprising and unexpected spiritual and emotional growth. And it can be the time when new relationships and opportunities come to us. This does not mean that we are attempting to interpret the death as a good thing, we are not falling into the temptation and common cliché of calling this death a blessing, the tragedy of death is usually anything but a blessing. But what we are saying is that even through a terrible event in our lives, some striking good can come. We need to be open to that good.

One of the most prevalent patterns of growth that often emerges in a person who has lost a loved one is the increased sense of empathy and compassion for others. When a person has suffered a great loss, when a person has deeply grieved, then it is far easier to understand and enter into the pain and heartache of others. Very often the most helpful people of all to those going through pain are those who have also been through deep and abiding hurt. When you can truly say to another, "I have been there," you have a credibility and integrity that cannot be overemphasized.

In our congregation some of those who have gone through the experience of death in the family have become such a beautiful support base for others. It has not been unusual for four or five who have lost spouses to do things together, to worship as a group, to spend much time with each other on the phone and in person. There is a sense of solidarity, of trust between them.

The Apostle Paul has written in 2 Corinthians 5:17, "If anyone is in Christ, he is a new creation, the old has passed away, behold the new has come." As Christ enters into our pain and sorrow, we do in fact become new people, and as such we can find a new sense of purpose and meaning in life. We do not short-circuit our grieving, we must walk that road in its entirety, but at the same time we become ever aware of the new growth and resurgence taking place within. Thus we can find some positive in the midst of the sorrow.

Let me make one further suggestion that might be helpful for those seeking to move on. I would suggest that you find at least three people that you can trust to help you walk down some new paths. Find three people, most likely those who have been through some pain in their lives, and have a strong sense of empathy and compassion. Find three people who have their feet firmly planted on the ground, who have a deep and abiding faith in Jesus Christ, and who are willing to give of themselves to others. Find people who are good listeners, who will put aside their own concerns long enough to give you the kind of support that you need. And if you cannot find these people, then ask your pastor or some other friend to help you find them. Congregations often have persons who have been trained in caring skills, these could serve as a resource to you.

Once you have discovered these three people, then share with them the specifics of the situation in which you find yourself. Be honest with them, let them know some of your joys and sorrows, your fears and hopes. Then also allow them to share with you something of their own story, how they have walked through their own pain and sorrow. But let them give you counsel about the future. You will make the final decisions, of course, about your own moving on, but listen to the collective wisdom of others.

The Christian community is such a valuable resource for us, for within most of our churches there are so many wise and loving and faithful people. There is such corporate faith and experience that goes far beyond what we might expect. We do not have to try and re-invent the wheel, we are not the first people going through this time of loss. Therefore, we need to learn to listen to others. Often it is best to choose three people who are not overly close to us, who are not emotionally tied into our situation or life. It may be easier for someone who is more removed to be more objective. Ask these friends to pray for you, to be there for you as you begin to chart your future. What a powerful resource such people can become!

So a time of death, a time of separation, can be a time of growth and open windows, instead of just watching all of the doors slamming shut. It can be a time of finding deep spiritual and emotional maturity that might not have been possible before that time. It may be a time of growing up into Christ, and then growing out to others. It may be a time of substantial growth.

2. A second word that can be stated with complete confidence during this time of transition is that God is with you. God did not cause this tragedy, God is not in the business of taking loved ones away from us. God in fact weeps with us, just as he did when Lazarus died. But God has promised to remain very close to us, to be with us in these times of uncertainty and pain. Whenever we are traveling on a new road, and we are not quite sure where we are and where we are going, we can be assured that God is with us; encouraging, guiding, supporting, loving.

Sometimes it is not very easy to see God at work in the present situation. Things seem to be so confusing, mixed up, blurred. We wonder where God is found in all of this, and why we cannot hear his voice. But often the best way to know what God is doing is to look at our past, to see how so often things have seemed to work together for good in some mysterious and positive way. Even when we look at the difficult past, we can often see how God was truly with us. We can even see how at those times when the doors seemed to be closed very tight, that suddenly God opened a new door of opportunity. When we look back, we can readily see so many ways that God's loving arms were around us.

Therefore, just as we can see how God was at work in the past, so we can also live in assurance and faith that He is working in the present. We can be convinced that just as God has never abandoned us in the past, so he never leaves us alone. In fact, it is often when we are most alone and hurt that God seems to be the closest to us. Jesus said the words of comfort, "Come unto me, all who are weary and heavy laden, and I will give you rest." God is with us every step of the way.

3. And then finally, the best is yet to come. One of the most dramatic and important promises that is given to those who follow Jesus Christ is that not even death can separate us from the love of Christ. In other words, it is telling us that the best is yet to come. There will come a day, it says in the book of Revelation, when he will wipe away every tear from our eyes, and death shall be no more, neither shall there be mourning nor crying nor pain and more, for the former things have passed away. (Rev. 21:4) The

best is yet to come, there will be a day when we shall be with Jesus Christ, there will come a day when death will be no more.

The same promise is given to us who are facing life. The best is yet to come. There are certainly times which seem exceptions to this, but for most of us God gives us so many new opportunities and possibilities for the future. The death of a loved one is not the end of our life, it does not mean that all hope and meaning is gone. Rather, we can rise again, we can experience Easter, we can find new life and hope and meaning. Jesus promised that we have not seen nor heard all the magnificent things God has in store for us. This promise is certainly not limited to some afterlife, it is meant for now.

A father of a friend of mine lost his wife some years ago. Because this man was up in his 70's, it would have been tempting for him to just give up on life. But he decided that life was still worth living, and so he would find a new direction to pursue. It was at that time that he discovered the joy of travel. Since that time almost every summer has found him traveling to Norway and other parts of Scandinavia, visiting relatives and friends, and looking forward more and more to his next trip every year.

He is now almost 90 years old, but he still travels every summer, staying overseas for a couple of months or more. He has faced several serious health problems, but nothing has been able to stop him from traveling. Not everyone can travel, of course, but there are many possibilities that can attract our interest and give us meaning and purpose.

So the best is yet to come. No matter what has happened to us, the Biblical message is that the best is yet to come. There is still a tomorrow, all of life has not been used up in yesterday. Jesus says to each of us, I came that you might have life and have it more abundantly. This does not only refer to the past, it also points to the future. So be open to the future, look for a way to serve others, find ways of giving and participating, be open to new doors swinging open. And always remember, the best is yet to come.

Personal Forms

Personal Information Form

Full name _____

Address _____

Birthplace _____ Birthdate _____

Social Security Number _____ Armed Forces serial No. _____

Name of spouse _____ Date of marriage _____

Name of next of kin (if not spouse) _____

Address _____

Father's name _____ Birthplace _____

Mother's name _____ (Mother's maiden name) _____

Mother's birthplace _____ Place of residence _____

Names, ages, and places of residence of children:

_____

_____

_____

Names, places of residence of brothers and sisters:

Employer _____

Schools attended _____

Church membership _____

Address of congregation _____

Work experiences:

Emergency Information Form

Name _____ Address _____

Social Security No. _____ Phone _____

Next of kin _____ Address _____

Relationship _____ Phone _____

Name of party to call in emergency _____ Phone _____

Name of doctor _____ Phone _____

Name of attorney _____ Phone _____

Name of accountant _____ Phone _____

Name of insurance agent _____ Phone _____

Name of stockbroker _____ Phone _____

Location of important papers:

Hospital and health insurance policies _____

Medicare number _____

Accident policies _____

Life insurance policies _____

Your will _____ Executor _____

Safety deposit box and key _____

House deed and all property papers _____

Bank accounts—both checking and savings (account numbers) _____

Loans outstanding _____

Securities (stocks, bonds, certificates) _____

Birth certificates _____ Income tax records _____

Car registration cards _____ Charge accounts _____

Burial plot ownership papers _____

Contents list of safety deposit box _____

_____

_____

Organ donation information _____

Funeral information (See "Instructions for My Family," in series of forms which follow.): _____

A LIVING WILL is an informed directive regarding the nature and extent of medical treatment in the event of a terminal illness or deterioration in health. Living Wills are not recognized by Minnesota statutes, but are increasingly used by health professionals and family members as a guide in determining the course of treatment for an individual.

The Living Will serves two primary purposes. It permits the individual to refuse treatment, but also eases the burden on family members to try to determine the person's intentions about the extent of medical intervention. A Living Will can be entered into before or after a medical diagnosis has been made.

LIVING WILL

TO MY FAMILY, MY PHYSICIAN, MY LAWYER, MY CLERGYMAN
TO ANY MEDICAL FACILITY IN WHOSE CARE I HAPPEN TO BE
TO ANY INDIVIDUAL WHO MAY BECOME RESPONSIBLE FOR MY HEALTH, WELFARE OR AFFAIRS

Death is as much a reality as birth, growth, maturity and old age— it is the one certainty of life. If the time comes when I, _____, can no longer take part in decisions for my own future, let this statement stand as an expression of my wishes, while I am still of sound mind.

If the situation should arise in which there is no reasonable expectation of my recovery from physical or mental disability, I request that I be allowed to die and not be kept alive by artificial means or "heroic measures". I do not fear death itself as much as the indignities of deterioration, dependence and hopeless pain. I, therefore, ask that medication be mercifully administered to me to alleviate suffering even though this may hasten the moment of death.

This request is made after careful consideration. I hope you who care for me will feel morally bound to follow its mandate. I recognize that this appears to place a heavy responsibility upon you, but it is with the intention of relieving you of such responsibility and of placing it upon myself in accordance with my strong convictions, that this statement is made.

Signed _____

Date _____

Witness _____

Witness _____

Copies of this request have been given to _____

_____

_____

_____

Instructions for My Family

I am providing these instructions in order to assist those making arrangements in the event of my death. I understand this is not a contract and is not binding on my family or estate.

A living will   Yes —————— No ——————

Autopsy   Yes —————— No ——————

Organ donation   Yes —————— No ——————

   If yes, which organs ——————————————

Name of funeral firm, memorial society or crematory society: ————————

City and State ————————————————————————

Reviewal of the body Yes —————— No ——————

Funeral service with casket —————— Memorial service without casket ——————

Place of funeral or memorial service ————————————————

Pastor ————————————————————————————

Memorials given to _____

Special arrangements for service (favorite hymn or scripture) _____

I prefer earth burial _____ Cremation _____

If burial, which cemetery _____

General casket description _____

Approximate cost of casket _____

Vault or liner _____ Approximate cost _____

Approximate total expense desired _____

(I understand that the prices indicated are current prices and that at the time of my death the prevailing market prices may be different.)

Special comments to my family _____

_____

Signed _____

Date _____

Organ and Body Donation

In the hope that I may help others, I hereby make this anatomical gift, if medically acceptable, to take effect upon my death. The words and marks below indicate my desires.

I give: (a) ☐ any needed organs or parts
(b) ☐ only the following organs or parts

_____
Specify which organ(s) or part(s)

for the purposes of transplantation, therapy, medical research or education;
(c) ☐ my body for anatomical study if needed.

_____
Limitations or special wishes, if any

Signed by the Donor and the following two witnesses in the presence of each other

_____ _____
Signature of Donor   Donor's Birthdate

_____ _____
City & State where signed   Date signed

_____ _____
Witness   Witness

This is a legal document under the Uniform Anatomical Gift Act or similar laws.

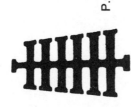

The Living Bank
P.O. Box 6725 • Houston, Texas 77265
713/528-2971

Uniform Donor Card

EMERGENCY

Keep this card with your driver's license

_____
Donor's Social Security No.

_____
Print or type next of kin & relationship

_____
Address of next of kin

_____
Phone of next of kin

FOR INFORMATION IN AN EMERGENCY, CONTACT THE LIVING BANK INTERNATIONAL, 713 / 528-2971

Adams, James. *The Sting of Death.*

Bachman, C. Charles. *Ministering to the Grief Sufferer.* Philadelphia: Fortress Press, 1964.

Bailey, Robert W. *Ministering to the Grieving.* Grand Rapids, Michigan: Zondervan, 1976.

Barnes, John. *Who Will Get Your Money?* New York: William Morrow & Company, 1972.

Bayly, Joseph. *The Last Thing We Talk About.* Elgin, Illinois: David C. Cook Publishing, 1969.

Bouman, Walter. Tape of Lectures at Holden Village. Chalen, Washington, 1977.

Burkett, Larry. *Your Finances in Changing Times.* Minneapolis: World Wide Publications, 1975.

Consumers Union. *Funerals: Consumers' Last Rights.* New York: W.W. Norton and Company, 1977.

Feifel, Herman. *New Meanings of Death.* New York: McGraw-Hill Book Company, 1977.

Irion, Paul E. *The Funeral and the Mourners.* Nashville: Abingdon Press, 1954, 1979.

Knudsen, Raymond B. *New Models for Creative Giving.* Chicago: Association Press, Follet Publishing, 1976.

Koch, Ron. *Goodbye Grandpa.* Minneapolis: Augsburg Publishing House, 1975.

Kubler-Ross, Elizabeth. *Death, The Final Stage of Growth.* Englewood Cliffs, NJ: Prentice-Hall, 1975.

Kubler-Ross, Elizabeth. *On Death and Dying.* London: The Macmillan Company, 1969.

Kushner, Harold S. *When Bad Things Happen to Good People.* New York: Avon Books, 1981.

Miller, William A. *When Going to Pieces Holds You Together.* Minneapolis: Augsburg Publishing House, 1976.

Mitford, Jessica. *The American Way of Death.* New York: Simon and Schuster, 1963.

Oates, Wayne E. *Pastoral Care and Counseling in Grief and Separation.* Philadelphia: Fortress Press, 1976.

Poovey, William A. *Planning the Christian Funeral.* Minneapolis: Augsburg Publishing House, 1978.

Riley, Miles O'Brien. *Set Your House in Order.* Garden City, NY: Doubleday and Company, 1980.

Rogness, Alvin N. *Appointment with Death.* Minneapolis: Augsburg Publishing House, 1968.

Rogness, Alvin N. *Book of Comfort.* Minneapolis: Augsburg Publishing House, 1979.

Sharpe, Robert F. *Everything You Wanted to Know Before You Give Another Dime.* Nashville: Thomas Nelson Publishers, 1979.

Simpson, Michael A. *The Facts of Death.* Englewood Cliffs, NJ: Prentice-Hall, Inc., 1979.

Tatelbaum, Judy. *The Courage to Grieve.* New York: Harper & Row, 1980.

Westberg, Granger E. *Good Grief.* Philadelphia: Fortress Press, 1971.

Williams, Phillip. *When a Loved One Dies.* Minneapolis: Augsburg Publishing House, 1978.

If you would like more information
about this book, or other books and video
available from Prince of Peace Publishing,
please write:

Prince of Peace Publishing, Inc.
13801 Fairview Drive
Burnsville, MN 55337

NOTES

DATE DUE			